STRATEGY EXECUTION

STRATEGY EXECUTION

THE ART OF ACHIEVING RESULTS

JAMES G. SMITH

GLENCOE
VENTURES

To my inspiration, Sarah,

Thank you for always believing in me and encouraging me to pursue my passions. Your unwavering support and love have been the driving force behind my work, and I could not have completed this book without you. Your intelligence, creativity, and kind heart continue to inspire me every day. This book is dedicated to you as a small token of my appreciation for all that you do. I hope it will bring you as much joy as you bring to my life.

With love and gratitude,

"Without strategy, execution is aimless. Without execution, strategy is useless."

Morris Chang, CEO of TSMC

CONTENTS

PREFACE

It was the start of a new year, and the leadership team was excited about their new strategy. They had spent months developing a plan that they believed would transform the organization and take it to the next level. It was a bold vision that had the potential to create significant value for all stakeholders.

But as the weeks and months went by, it became apparent that something was not right. Despite the enthusiasm and the resources allocated, the execution of the strategy was not going as planned. Progress was slow, and there were missed deadlines and unmet targets. The leadership team was frustrated, and morale began to wane.

This scenario is not uncommon. In fact, it is all too familiar to many organizations. The reality is that many strategies fail not because they are flawed, but because of poor execution. It is the Achilles heel of many businesses, and the consequences can be dire.

As a business leader, I've observed the outcomes of strategy execution - both successes and failures. From my experience, I've learned that executing a strategy isn't just about having a plan; it requires balance, discipline, focus, and the right culture. In this book, practical advice is shared on how to successfully design, develop, and implement a strategy meant to last. This includes establishing frameworks for strategy execution, creating a culture, developing a committed and accountable team, tracking progress, listening to market conditions, and making adjustments when necessary.

The book also features stories of companies that have both succeeded and failed at strategy execution, providing valuable insights into best practices and challenges. By understanding these experiences, we can equip ourselves to drive organizational success.

Just as building a house requires a blueprint, a solid foundation, and a team of skilled workers to bring it to life, strategy execution requires a well-designed plan, a strong organizational culture, and a team of motivated employees to make it happen.

The blueprint represents the strategic plan, outlining the steps and resources needed to achieve the desired outcome. The foundation is the organizational culture, which sets the tone for how work gets done and how employees behave. Without a strong foundation, the house (or strategy) may crumble under pressure.

The team of skilled workers represents the employees responsible for executing the strategy. Just as each worker has a specific job to do, each employee plays a unique role in the execution of the strategy. Without the right team in place, the house (or strategy) may never be completed.

Overall, strategy execution requires careful planning, a solid foundation, and a motivated team to turn the plan into a successful reality, much like building a house.

PART I

THE IMPORTANCE OF STRATEGY EXECUTION

Let's take a moment to assess our current position regarding strategy before delving into the book's content. Presumably, you have picked up this book with the intention of improving some aspect of your organization. Perhaps you want to reinforce your existing strategy, gain a new perspective on the subject, or acknowledge that your organization lacks a strategy altogether, and is therefore on a path towards failure.

However, let's hope that things are not that dire. To begin, we will conduct a review, and I urge you to ask yourselves the following questions. We will revisit these questions and others throughout the book to gain insight into your organization's current state of strategy development and its readiness to execute the strategy.

Do You Have a Well-Developed Strategy?

- Is there a documented strategy that is communicated throughout the organization?
- Does the strategy align with the organization's mission, vision, and values?

1

THE AGONY OF DEFEAT

The clock was ticking down, and the tension in the stadium was palpable. With just seconds left on the clock, the Seattle Seahawks were on the brink of history. They were about to win their second consecutive Super Bowl championship, cementing their place in NFL history as one of the greatest teams of all time. But in a split second decision that would haunt them for years to come, everything changed.

The Seahawks had the ball on the New England Patriots' 1-yard line, with just 26 seconds left on the clock and trailing by four points. It was a crucial moment, and everyone in the stadium knew it. The Seahawks had a star running back in Marshawn Lynch, who had been dominating the game with his powerful running style. He was the obvious choice to carry the ball and score the game-winning touchdown.

But in a shocking move, the Seahawks coaching staff decided to go for a pass play instead. They called for a quick slant pass to wide receiver Ricardo Lockette, hoping to catch the Patriots off guard and score the touchdown. It was a bold move, but it would prove to be their downfall.

As the ball was snapped, the tension in the stadium reached a fever pitch. The Seahawks quarterback, Russell Wilson, dropped back to pass and fired the ball towards Lockette. But before he could even get his hands on it, the Patriots cornerback Malcolm Butler jumped in front of him and intercepted the pass.

The stadium erupted in disbelief. The Seahawks had just lost the Super Bowl in the most dramatic fashion possible. The coaching staff's decision to throw the ball instead of giving it to Lynch would be heavily criticized in the aftermath of the game. It was a failure of strategy execution on the grandest stage imaginable.

In the Seahawks locker room after the game, there was a stunned silence. The players and coaching staff were devastated. They knew that they had let a historic opportunity slip away, and it was a bitter pill to swallow. The agony of defeat was written on their faces, and it would stay with them for a long time to come.

In the end, the failure of strategy execution in Super Bowl XLIX would be a lesson for all to learn from. It showed that even the best-laid plans can fail if they are not executed properly. It demonstrated the importance of situational awareness, strategic decision-making, and proper execution in sports and in life. And it would serve as a reminder to never take anything for granted, especially in the high-stakes world of professional sports.

Errors in execution, such as the one made by the Seattle Seahawks in Super Bowl XLIX, can happen due to a variety of reasons. Sometimes, emotions and pressure can cloud judgment and cause individuals to make decisions that go against their better judgment. In other cases, overthinking and second-guessing can lead to indecision and missed opportunities. Moreover, lack of communication, coordination, and preparation can also lead to errors in execution.

In the case of the Seahawks, the coaching staff's decision to throw the ball instead of handing it off to Marshawn Lynch was a result of overthinking and over-analyzing the situation. They thought they had the element of surprise on their side, but they failed to consider the risks associated with the pass play, such as the possibility of an interception. Moreover, they underestimated the Patriots' defense, which was well-prepared for such a scenario.

What the Seahawks should have done instead was to stick to their game plan and run the ball with Lynch. Lynch had been their best offensive player throughout the game, and he had been successful in short-yardage situations. The Seahawks coaching staff should have trusted their star player and given him the ball in that critical moment. It was a safer and more reliable option that would have given them a greater chance of success.

2

STRATEGY VS. STRATEGY EXECUTION

W e know their names; Kodak, Blockbuster, Sears, Nokia. All were once renowned and prosperous. Known by virtually everyone. Despite having achieved a position of dominance in their respective markets, they are now referenced in the past tense. We are left to ponder why they fell from grace and examine the reasons behind their failures. After all, each of these organizations had a well-defined strategy, so what crucial element were they lacking?

When it comes to business, the words "strategy" and "strategy execution" are frequently used interchangeably, but they denote two separate stages in reaching organizational objectives. Crafting a carefully thought-out strategy is essential for any organization to succeed, but it is only the initial phase in a lengthy process of accomplishing business objectives. Equally important is strategy execution, which involves implementing the plan and attaining the desired results. It is the reason why even companies as dominant as Kodak can falter - they had a strategy, but failed to execute it effectively.

"Strategy" and "Strategy Execution" are related concepts but refer to different stages in the process of achieving business goals.

Strategy refers to the process of setting a direction or plan to achieve specific business objectives. It involves analyzing the market, identifying opportunities and threats, and developing a comprehensive plan to achieve long-term goals. Strategy involves making decisions about where to focus resources, which markets to target, and which products or services to offer.

On the other hand, Strategy Execution refers to the process of implementing the strategy to achieve business goals. It involves putting the plan into action, monitoring progress, making adjustments as needed, and ensuring that everyone in the organization is aligned and working towards the same goals. Strategy Execution involves translating the strategy into concrete actions and ensuring that those actions are carried out effectively.

Strategy execution is more than just developing a plan, it is the critical process of turning a vision into reality. It involves aligning resources, people, and processes towards a common goal and ensuring that everyone in the organization is working towards the same objective. Successful strategy execution requires a deep understanding of the business landscape, the ability to anticipate potential roadblocks, and the agility to pivot when necessary. It is the glue that holds together a company's mission and values with its day-to-day operations, and it is what separates successful organizations from those that struggle to achieve their goals. In short, strategy execution is the key to transforming a great idea into a thriving business.

There are likely countless organizations that have experienced a comparable defeat to Kodak. Moreover, there may be companies that are presently operational and appear to be doing well, but are most likely executing at only 75% of their potential. Imagine if those thousands of companies increased their executional output by 5% or 10%. Imagine all the mangers that might have made their year end bonus, instead of missing it by a small fraction.

The development of a solid strategy is a critical component of business success, and leaders should prioritize it accordingly. Unfortunately, there are many reasons why strategy development and execution does not receive the level of attention it so desperately deserves.

We've witnessed it countless times - a company carefully crafts a sound strategy, but when Q2 results fall slightly short of expectations, leadership abandons the original plan and mandates short-term fixes to boost results. This approach completely disregards the previously developed strategy and often leads to repeated attempts to implement a new one the following year, with similar results. This approach can lead to missed opportunities and ultimately hinder the organization's long-term growth.

Have you ever found yourself in a situation where you are completely swamped with work? You feel overwhelmed by the number of tasks you need to complete and are already working nights and weekends just to keep up. Then suddenly, your boss drops new initiatives on your plate without removing any of your already overwhelming responsibilities. Unfortunately, this lack of resources is another significant obstacle that can prevent leaders from dedicating time to developing a sound strategy or executing an existing one.

When teams are already overburdened with work and have limited resources, it can be challenging to prioritize strategy development. There may be competing demands for time, and team members may not have the necessary bandwidth to devote to strategic planning or execution. Additionally, limited resources can also lead to a lack of access to critical data or expertise, further hampering the ability to develop a comprehensive strategy.

However, it is essential to recognize that neglecting strategy development can have significant long-term consequences for the organization. Without a clear and comprehensive strategy, the organization may struggle to remain competitive, achieve its goals, or respond effectively to changing market conditions. As such, leaders need to find ways to allocate the necessary resources, whether it be by prioritizing strategic planning or investing in additional resources, to ensure that the organization can develop and execute a sound strategy.

There is a growing trend of companies getting rid of meetings, and the reason behind it is that many leaders have become overly preoccupied with day-to-day operations and tasks, leaving them with little time to focus on strategy execution. The phrase "this meeting could have been an email" has become popular due to the frustration of employees who feel their time is being wasted in meetings that are not productive or relevant to their work. As a result, some companies are reducing the number of meetings or even eliminating them altogether, allowing leaders and employees to focus on more critical tasks, such as executing the company's strategy. By doing so, companies can ensure that they are making the most of their time and resources, ultimately leading to improved business performance and success.

How do leaders' resistance to change affect strategy execution? Fear of change is a real phenomenon that can hinder the success of an organization. It is not uncommon for leaders to feel apprehensive about making changes to their organization's structure or processes, even if it means improving strategy execution. The mere mention of the word "change" can send some running for the hills.

Overcoming resistance to change is not an easy task, but it is necessary for organizations to evolve and execute their strategies successfully. Leaders must be willing to embrace change and recognize its potential benefits. They must communicate the need for change effectively to employees and provide support and resources to help them adapt to new ways of working.

Ignoring the need for change can lead to missed opportunities, stagnation, and ultimately, failure. Therefore, leaders must understand that change is inevitable and necessary for growth and success. By embracing change and promoting a culture of continuous improvement, leaders can create an environment that encourages strategy execution and ultimately leads to sustained success for the organization.

Developing a clear and comprehensive strategy is a critical component of achieving long-term success for any organization. It provides a roadmap for the organization, outlining the goals and objectives, as well as the steps needed to achieve them. This not only helps to ensure that everyone is working towards the same objectives, but it also helps to identify potential roadblocks or challenges along the way, allowing for proactive planning and mitigation.

While developing a comprehensive strategy may require significant time, effort, and resources, the long-term benefits are undeniable. By providing clear direction and guidance, a solid strategy can help organizations achieve sustained success and growth, even in the face of challenges and uncertainty.

3

RETURN ON MANAGEMENT

Cash reigns supreme when it comes to valuable assets within an organization. This is because cash holds the versatility to be converted into any other asset such as inventory, advertising, office supplies, labor, and more. As a result, cash is highly prized for its ability to procure all the necessities required to run a successful business. But if cash is the most valuable asset. What is the most precious asset to a company?

Management's time and attention are the most precious assets of an organization because they are finite and irreplaceable. Unlike cash, which can be replenished through fundraising or investment, management's time and attention are limited resources that cannot be replenished once they have been expended.

Effective management requires careful allocation of time and attention to the most critical activities that drive long-term success. This includes setting clear strategic objectives, allocating resources effectively, managing risk, and building a strong culture and team. Failure to prioritize these activities can lead to wasted resources, missed opportunities, and even the failure of the organization.

Moreover, management's time and attention are also critical for fostering innovation and adaptation in the organization. In today's rapidly changing business environment, organizations must be able to adapt quickly to new challenges and opportunities. This requires management's time and attention to be focused on identifying emerging trends and technologies, experimenting with new ideas, and cultivating a culture of innovation and experimentation.

Return on management (ROM) is a concept that measures the effectiveness of a company's management team in creating value for the organization. It is similar to the more commonly known return on investment (ROI) concept, which measures the financial return. The ROM concept recognizes that a company's success is not just a function of its financial performance, but also the quality of its management. A strong management team can help to drive innovation, attract top talent, optimize resources, and manage risk effectively. In contrast, poor management can lead to missed opportunities, organizational inefficiencies, and other problems that can negatively impact a company's financial performance.

In a world of unlimited opportunities, organizations are often faced with a wide range of potential initiatives, investments, and growth opportunities. However, not all opportunities are created equal, and management's time and attention are finite resources. Therefore, it is critical for organizations to prioritize their efforts and allocate management's time and attention to the most valuable initiatives that drive long-term success. ROM provides a framework for measuring the value of management's time and attention by evaluating the effectiveness of management's decisions and actions. By measuring the impact of management's efforts on the organization's financial performance, ROM can help organizations identify areas of improvement and optimize their use of management's time and attention.

Moreover, ROM can help organizations to make better decisions about where to allocate resources and which initiatives to pursue. By prioritizing initiatives with the highest ROM, organizations can ensure that they are maximizing the value of their resources and driving sustainable growth over the long term.

$$ROM = \frac{\text{Productive organizational energy released}}{\text{Management time and attention invested}}$$

Let's start by clarifying that ROM is not a quantitative formula that produces a specific number or percentage. Rather, it is a qualitative measure that requires managers to interpret and estimate both the numerator and denominator, as well as the overall outcome. The purpose of ROM is to provide a directional indication of management's effectiveness. Like other quantitative return ratios, ROM is maximized when the numerator is large and the denominator is small. Using this ratio, managers can determine if their ROM is high, medium, or low, although it is only a rough estimate. Nonetheless, it has been found that executives who grasp the value of ROM possess a powerful tool for comprehending and catalyzing change.

Let's consider two fictitious companies to illustrate how ROM works. The first company, TechX, is a small tech consultancy based in San Francisco. They started with a clear strategy of providing cloud-based solutions to startups. TechX quickly gained recognition for their expertise and expanded to four offices across the US. However, after seven years, the company was in dire straits. In one office, staff were discovered to be cross-charging clients to meet budget requirements. In another office, management had failed to notice a decline in business generated by three of the company's largest clients, leaving many professionals idle. In a third office, an attempt to automate a client's software system resulted in financial losses and embarrassment as the consultancy realized it lacked the skills to deliver the project.

To put it simply, the organization had fallen apart. The management team was trying to tackle too many projects, clients, and objectives without any clear priorities. Initially, the company had a solid and concentrated strategy centered around delivering cutting-edge industrial technology to its clients. However, the managers allowed themselves to get sidetracked by the numerous possibilities presented to them, which diverted their attention away from executing the core strategy. As a result, the organization's productive output was minimal, despite the significant investment of management time. Consequently, the company's ROM was abysmal.

On the other hand, Zenith Analytics, a large data processing company headquartered in Boston, is an example of a company where managers understand the value of focusing their energy on projects that align with their strategy. By using a strict checklist to evaluate whether a project aligns with the company's strategy and clearly communicating their priorities, Zenith Analytics achieved 35 years of consecutive double-digit growth, a record unmatched by any other company. This success is due to the disciplined approach to energy allocation where managers make hard choices about where to commit their energy and where not to, instead of trying to capture every opportunity that comes their way.

The distinguishing factor between these two companies is straightforward: Zenith Analytic's managers concentrate their efforts on specific, well-defined strategic priorities, only investing time once they perceive the ability to achieve the desired results. While both companies' managers recognize the abundance of business opportunities available, Zenith Analytic's managers understand that there are only so many hours in a day and a limited number of managers available. Like all high-ROM managers, they recognize that organizations prosper when their leaders and employees are disciplined about how they utilize their time. Instead of attempting to pursue every opportunity, like TechX did, they make tough decisions about where to devote their energy, and, more importantly, where not to. This clarity of purpose transforms all energy into productive energy and propels the company's strategy from the boardroom to the marketplace.

4

WHY MANY ORGANIZATIONS FAIL

People can learn from studying both success and failure. Success can provide valuable feedback on what works well and can be replicated in the future. However, success may also lead to complacency and a reluctance to change or adapt to new challenges. On the other hand, studying others' failures can provide valuable insights into what not to do and what mistakes to avoid. By examining the reasons behind the failures of others, individuals and organizations can learn from those mistakes and apply those lessons learned to their own strategies and operations. Additionally, studying others' failures can help individuals and organizations identify potential risks and challenges that they may not have considered before.

Strategy is a critical component of an organization's success, and failure to execute a strategy can have significant consequences. While we do tend to study organizations that fail spectacularly, typically shuttering completely. It is more important to think of the multitude of organizations that are operating year over year, but only at 70% of their potential. For every failed business we study, there are arguably hundreds or thousands of others that are operating below potential.

Operating below full potential is not a welcome option, especially in the sport of Formula One racing. The rate at which Formula One cars improve from year to year varies based on several factors, such as changes in regulations, technology advancements, and competition levels. However, the top Formula One teams are estimated to spend upward of $400 million per year looking to improve their car's performance. So how much does $400 million buy in Formula One? In the 2020 season, the Mercedes team improved their car's performance by approximately 0.5 seconds per lap compared to the previous year's car, which helped them secure their seventh consecutive Constructors' Championship.

$400 million buys 1/2 second

Imagine if you could approach Mercedes and tell them you could help them improve operations 1%. Or 5% for that matter. That small of a jump could mean years of improvement and success for the team.

～

THERE ARE many individuals types of businesses in the world, and it's impossible to go over every single area of risk. There are some common elements that most businesses share where we can start taking a look at our own strategies, and evaluate if they are working or if there are opportunities for improvement.

Alignment. A lack of alignment between the strategy and the organization's mission and vision means that the strategy may not be relevant or valuable to the organization. For example, if an organization's mission is to provide high-quality, affordable healthcare to underserved communities, but the strategy focuses on expanding to wealthy communities, then there is a lack of alignment between the strategy and the organization's mission. This can lead to confusion, silos, and wasted effort as team members may not understand how their work supports the organization's mission and vision.

Poor Communications. Leaders need to communicate the strategy clearly, consistently, and in a way that is relevant to their audience. They need to ensure that everyone understands the goals, the execution plan, their role, and how success will be measured. Effective communication can build buy-in, engagement, and commitment to the strategy, while poor communication can hinder progress and lead to failure.

Lack of Leadership. If leaders are not bought into the strategy, it can be difficult to get the rest of the organization to be committed as well. Leaders play a critical role in setting the tone and direction for the organization, so if they are not on board with the strategy, it is unlikely to be successful. To overcome this challenge, leadership must buy-in early and communicate the strategy's importance to the entire organization.

Inadequate Resources. Without the right resources, it's difficult to implement the strategy effectively. This can include a lack of financial resources, such as funding for new technology or equipment, or a lack of human resources, such as staffing or expertise. Additionally, inadequate technology can make it difficult to execute the strategy efficiently.

Poor Planning. Without a clear execution plan, it can be difficult to measure progress and allocate resources effectively. This can lead to confusion and wasted effort, as well as missed opportunities to pivot and make necessary adjustments to stay on track. A well-crafted execution plan helps to ensure that everyone in the organization is on the same page, and understands their role and what needs to be done to execute the strategy effectively.

Inadequate Tracking. If an organization doesn't set up an effective tracking and measurement system, it won't be able to know whether the strategy is being executed effectively or not. Without these metrics, it is difficult to evaluate progress or identify areas that require improvement. This can lead to a lack of accountability, where team members may not feel responsible for their part in executing the strategy. Furthermore, without tracking and measurement, it is impossible to make informed decisions or course corrections as necessary.

Resistance to Change. If people are not willing to embrace the changes required to execute the strategy, it can impede progress and result in a lack of engagement from team members. Overcoming resistance to change requires effective communication, involvement of key stakeholders, and a clear understanding of the benefits of the strategy.

Overall, strategy execution is complex, and there are many factors that can contribute to its success or failure within an organization. It is vital organizations address these factors and develop a clear plan for executing their strategy in order to increase the likelihood of success.

PART II

DEFINING YOUR STRATEGY

Let's reassess the viability of your organization's strategy. How confident are you that it will lead to success? It's important to acknowledge that having a well-crafted strategy does not guarantee success. Success is contingent upon various factors such as effective execution, adaptability to changes in the external environment, and resource availability.

- Has your strategy been communicated effectively throughout the organization?
- Are the resources necessary to execute your strategy available?
- Is there a plan in place to monitor and measure the progress of the strategy?
- Are there contingency plans in place in case the external environment changes?

5

THE FOUR LEVERS OF CONTROL

The Four Levers of Control framework is a management model that helps organizations establish and maintain effective control systems. The framework was developed by Robert Simons, a professor at Harvard Business School, and it emphasizes the importance of balancing the need for control with the need for flexibility and innovation (Simons, 1995). The framework consists of four levers of control: Belief Systems, Boundary Systems, Diagnostic Control Systems, and Interactive Control Systems. By understanding and utilizing these levers, organizations can effectively align their strategies, goals, and actions to achieve success.

Simons observed that many companies were relying too heavily on financial controls to manage their organizations, which could lead to short-term thinking and a lack of focus on long-term strategic objectives. Simons' framework proposed a more holistic approach to management, incorporating four key "levers of control" to help companies achieve their strategic goals.

- Belief Systems: The values, beliefs, and culture of
  the organization. It is the foundation upon which
  the other levers of control are built.
- Boundary Systems: The rules, policies, and
  procedures that guide employee behavior and
  ensure compliance with legal and ethical standards.
- Diagnostic Control Systems: The performance
  metrics, key performance indicators (KPIs), and
  other data-driven tools that help managers monitor
  progress and identify areas that require attention.
- Interactive Control Systems: The communication
  channels and feedback mechanisms that facilitate
  collaboration and alignment across the
  organization.

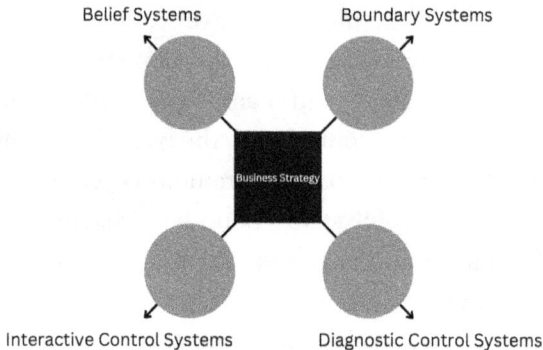

Belief Systems   Boundary Systems

Business Strategy

Interactive Control Systems   Diagnostic Control Systems

The Four Levers of Control

Belief Systems

Within a business, belief systems are utilized to convey an organization's vision, mission, and core values. These belief systems
effectively communicate what the business aims to accomplish
and how employees should interact with one another, clients,

suppliers, and the broader society. Belief systems are highly influential in guiding people and providing them with a sense of purpose. Although many companies prominently display their values, integrating these values into daily conversations can be a challenging task.

Core values, which are the fundamental beliefs and principles that guide the behavior and decision-making of an organization, represent the company's identity, purpose, and principles. Core values reflect the organization's culture and are essential for establishing and maintaining a cohesive and productive work environment.

Well-defined core values provide a sense of direction and purpose for employees, helping them understand what the company is striving to achieve. Core values can also help to attract and retain employees who share similar beliefs and principles, leading to a more committed and engaged workforce. Furthermore, core values can guide decision-making, particularly in ambiguous or challenging circumstances, by providing a framework for evaluating options and making decisions that align with the organization's principles. Core values play a crucial role in establishing a clear identity and culture, guiding employee behavior and decision-making, and attracting and retaining a committed and engaged workforce.

Patagonia, an outdoor clothing and gear company, serves as an exemplary model for a company with strong belief systems. Their mission statement, "We're in business to save our home planet," reflects their dedication to environmental sustainability, which is also evident in their values such as "Build the best product," "Cause no unnecessary harm," and "Use business to protect nature." These values are ingrained in their products, marketing, and actions, including donating 1% of their sales to environmental causes and advocating for the protection of public lands.

Another company with a well-defined belief system is Starbucks, whose mission statement is "to inspire and nurture the human spirit – one person, one cup, and one neighborhood at a time." They also have a set of core values, including a commitment to "creating a culture of warmth and belonging," "acting with courage and finding new ways to grow our company and each other," and "being present, connecting with transparency, dignity, and respect." These values are communicated to employees and customers, helping to create a recognizable brand identity for the company.

Boundary Systems

To enhance focus and prevent unproductive distractions, boundary systems define what an organization will not engage in. This may seem counterintuitive, but by narrowing down the activities, the company can concentrate on the opportunities that align with their objectives. Furthermore, boundary systems play a critical role in defining a company's unique value proposition. This proposition communicates to potential customers the benefits of the product or service compared to its competitors. By identifying what they won't do, companies can clarify what sets them apart.

Additionally, boundary systems are an essential tool to address potential risks. Risks can jeopardize the company's financial stability, reputation, customer satisfaction, employee morale, and legal compliance. By identifying and avoiding these risks, boundary systems help to protect the organization's interests and ensure its long-term success.

Companies face various types of risks that they must avoid or manage. Financial risks are related to cash flow, credit, investments, and foreign exchange. Operational risks are associated with the company's daily operations, including product quality, supply chain disruptions, and IT failures. Legal and regulatory risks involve compliance with laws and regulations, such as data privacy, environmental regulations, and workplace safety. Non-compliance can result in fines, legal action, and reputational damage. Reputational risks arise from negative publicity, such as product recalls, data breaches, or ethical misconduct, which can lead to decreased sales, loss of customers, and difficulty attracting and retaining talent.

Recall the early days of Netflix. The business model catered to sending DVDs via mail. Their business model allowed customers to create a personalized playlist of movies online, and Netflix would send DVDs one at a time via mail to the customer. While this approach may seem outdated now, it exemplifies how a business can establish a boundary to focus its strategy. By stating that they were not going to focus on the physical DVD rental business any longer, Netflix was able to shift their resources and efforts towards developing streaming technology and building a streaming library. This strategic decision ultimately led to their success in the streaming market and helped them become the dominant player in the industry, leaving Blockbuster behind.

Diagnostic Control Systems

Diagnostic controls are often associated with the concept of strategy, as they involve outlining the processes, tasks, and milestones that are integral to achieving organizational objectives. These controls utilize performance measures to provide feedback on how well the organization is meeting its targets. The primary focus of diagnostic controls is measurement, with an emphasis on identifying variances from the desired outcomes and taking corrective action. Formal meetings, such as those held by departments, teams, and the board, are typically used to review performance and ensure that progress is being effectively managed and tracked.

While tasks and milestones are commonly associated with

diagnostic controls, there are various other examples of diagnostic controls that can be used as part of an organization's strategy.

- Financial ratios: Diagnostic controls such as current ratio, quick ratio, and debt-to-equity ratio enable companies to monitor their financial performance and make informed decisions based on the results.
- Sales reports: Sales reports provide diagnostic control over a company's sales performance, enabling them to track trends, compare results to forecasts, and adjust sales strategies accordingly.
- Customer satisfaction surveys: Companies reliant on customer loyalty and repeat business use customer satisfaction surveys as a critical diagnostic control. By gathering regular feedback from customers and using the results to make improvements, companies can increase customer satisfaction and retention.
- Quality control measures: Diagnostic controls such as statistical process control, inspection procedures, and product testing help companies monitor and enhance the quality of their products or services.
- Performance appraisals: Performance appraisals are a prevalent diagnostic control used to evaluate employee performance and identify areas for improvement. This allows companies to create training programs, provide feedback to employees, and enhance overall organizational performance.
- Operational reviews: Operational reviews are a diagnostic control that allows companies to analyze their operations and identify areas for improvement. This includes scrutinizing processes, procedures, and systems to identify inefficiencies and develop solutions to enhance performance.

Diagnostic Controls play a crucial role in managing Critical Performance Variables (CPVs) of a company. These CPVs are specific metrics that are used to measure and evaluate the performance of an organization. Typically, these variables are closely linked to the organization's strategic objectives and are the most important drivers of success. By measuring and monitoring these variables, businesses can assess whether they are meeting their goals, identify areas for improvement, and make data-driven decisions.

The critical performance variables for a business or organization can vary depending on its nature, but they usually include metrics such as revenue growth, profitability, customer satisfaction, employee productivity, and the quality of products or services. Monitoring these variables allows businesses to identify trends, strengths, and weaknesses, and to develop strategies to improve overall performance. Furthermore, continuously measuring and monitoring CPVs provides a framework for ongoing improvement, which is essential in a highly competitive business environment where changes occur rapidly.

Amazon is known for its data-driven approach to business, and it leverages advanced analytics and metrics to evaluate the performance of its operations, products, and services. For example, Amazon uses its diagnostic control systems to monitor and optimize its supply chain operations. The company tracks metrics such as inventory levels, shipping times, and delivery costs, and uses this data to identify areas where it can improve efficiency and reduce costs. By implementing changes based on these metrics, Amazon has been able to streamline its supply chain and offer faster and more reliable delivery to its customers.

Amazon's diagnostic control systems also play a critical role in its product development and marketing strategies. The company tracks customer data, such as purchase history and browsing behavior, to identify trends and preferences, and uses this information to develop targeted marketing campaigns, personalize product recommendations, and move inventory amongst their distribution centers to ensure fast delivery when an order is made.

Interactive Control Systems

Interactive Controls are a management approach that promotes ongoing and two-way communication between senior management, all levels of the organization, and the customer base. The purpose is to address critical issues or objectives that are important for the success of the company. This approach involves regular questioning and feedback to ensure that progress is being made and that any problems or issues are identified and addressed promptly. Interactive Controls help to ensure that all members of the organization are aligned and working towards a common goal while providing clarity on what is expected of them in achieving that goal.

Strategic uncertainty is associated with the unpredictability and unknowns that are part of a company's long-term strategy and external environment. By using Interactive Controls, companies can uncover and manage strategic uncertainty effectively. This helps them prepare for potential disruptions, identify new opportunities, and make informed decisions. By doing so, companies can maintain their competitive edge, adapt to changing market conditions, and minimize risks while maximizing opportunities for growth and success.

An example of a company using interactive controls as part of their strategy is Toyota. The Japanese automaker uses a management approach called the "Toyota Production System" which is focused on continuous improvement and eliminating waste in the production process. As part of this approach,

Toyota employs a system called "Andon" which allows any employee to stop the production line if they identify a problem that needs to be addressed. This creates a culture of communication and problem-solving at all levels of the organization, and ensures that issues are addressed in a timely manner to minimize downtime and waste. Additionally, Toyota's senior management regularly visits production facilities to observe operations and engage with employees, providing an opportunity for two-way communication and feedback. This approach has helped Toyota maintain a competitive edge in the automotive industry by continuously improving its processes and products.

The Four Levers of Control Model

The Four Levers of Control model involves balancing four types of control levers to achieve effective management control. Each lever has a specific function and must interact with the others to maintain balance within the strategy, ensuring the organization's success.

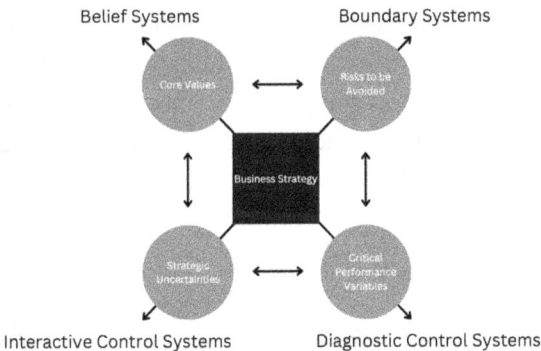

The Interaction within the Four Levers of Control (Simons, 2016)

Benefits of Using the Four Levers of Control

The four levers of control model offers a set of guidelines that can help organizations to achieve a range of benefits.

- Improved alignment is one of these benefits, as the model ensures that all parts of the organization are working towards the same strategic goals.
- Better communication is also promoted, as the model can establish clear channels of communication to prevent misunderstandings and ensure that everyone is working towards the same objectives.
- Increased accountability is another benefit, as the model emphasizes the need for regular monitoring and reporting of performance to ensure that everyone is working to the same standards.
- The model encourages organizations to be adaptable and responsive to changing circumstances, promoting enhanced flexibility through a framework for regular review and adjustment of strategy and operations.
- Finally, the model provides a systematic approach to decision-making, which can help organizations to make better-informed decisions based on a clear understanding of their objectives and the risks and opportunities involved.

Pitfalls to be Avoided

While the four levers of control model provides a comprehensive framework for organizations to implement effective control systems. There are several potential pitfalls to be aware of to ensure the model is used to its full potential.

- Over-reliance on a single lever can lead to an incomplete or ineffective approach to control. The model emphasizes the importance of using all four levers in combination to achieve the desired results.
- The levers should be aligned with the company's overall strategy. Regular review and updating of the levers is crucial to ensure they continue to support the business objectives.
- The levers should be consistently applied across the organization to ensure everyone is on the same page and working towards the same goals. Inconsistencies can lead to confusion and a lack of accountability.
- While the levers provide a framework for control, they should not be too rigid or inflexible. Being open to new ideas and making adjustments to the levers as necessary is essential to adapt to changing circumstances.
- Ignoring feedback from all levels of the organization can lead to a breakdown in the effectiveness of the levers. The levers are designed to be responsive to feedback, and it's important to actively seek and incorporate feedback to ensure they remain effective.

Balancing the Strategy

The Four Levers of Control model aims to strike a balance between constraining and guiding individuals' actions in an organization. It achieves this balance by using boundary systems and diagnostic controls as the **constraining levers** that limit behavior and guide decision-making.

By defining the milestones, processes, KPIs, and unique value propositions, these levers not only inform the organization what they should do, they are more importantly giving focus to the organization by eliminating the unlimited number of other opportunities to the organization. These levers tell us what NOT TO DO.

On the other hand, belief systems and interactive controls act as the **guiding levers** that help individuals to comprehend and internalize the organization's vision, values, and goals. These levers enhance our awareness and informing our decision making. These levers tell us what TO DO.

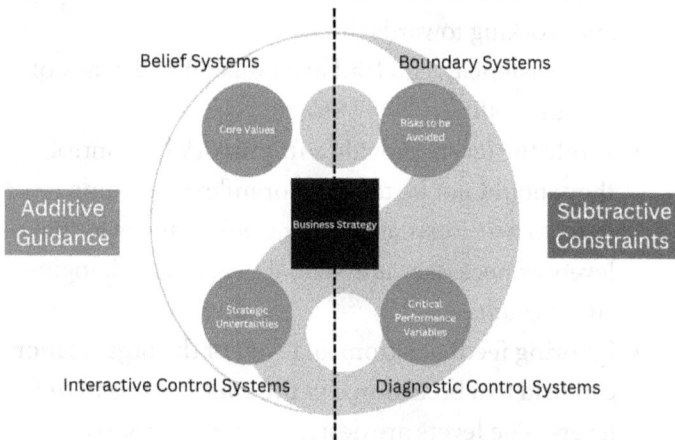

Belief Systems

Boundary Systems

Core Values

Risks to be Avoided

Additive Guidance

Business Strategy

Subtractive Constraints

Strategic Uncertainties

Critical Performance Variables

Interactive Control Systems

Diagnostic Control Systems

The Balance Within the Four Levers of Control

It is important to maintain a balance between these levers of control to avoid over-constraining or over-guiding individuals in the organization. If the constraining levers are too strict, it can stifle innovation and creativity, leading to a lack of adaptability in the face of changing circumstances. On the other hand, if the guiding levers are too loose, it can lead to confusion and lack of focus on the organization's goals and values. Therefore, the balance between the four levers is crucial for effective implementation.

How can I use the Four Levers

Let's take a moment to evaluate your organization's strategy using this model.

Let's first consider belief systems. Does your organization have a clear and defined set of beliefs that guide its operations? Are these beliefs effectively communicated to employees and stakeholders? Do they align with the organization's goals and values? If so, this is a positive element of your organization's strategy.

Next, let's look at boundary systems. Are there clear boundaries that define the scope of your organization's operations? Are these boundaries effective in guiding decision-making and resource allocation? Do they allow for flexibility and innovation within the organization? If there are any issues with your organization's boundary systems, these should be addressed to ensure that the strategy is effective.

Thirdly, let's consider diagnostic control systems. Does your organization have effective systems in place for measuring and monitoring performance? Are these systems aligned with the organization's goals and objectives? Do they provide meaningful insights that can be used to make informed decisions? If your organization has effective diagnostic control systems, this is a positive element of your strategy.

Finally, let's look at interactive control systems. Does your organization have effective communication channels and decision-making processes in place? Are employees empowered to contribute ideas and suggestions? Is there a culture of collaboration and accountability within the organization? If so, this is a positive element of your organization's strategy.

Take a moment to reflect on your organization's strategy and evaluate each of these four elements. What elements are going well, and what elements could be improved upon? Are there any areas where the organization's strategy is lacking? By evaluating your organization's strategy using the Four Levers of Control model, you can identify areas for improvement and develop a more effective strategy that leads to success.

6

BELIEF SYSTEMS

B elief systems refer to the shared values, norms, and beliefs that shape an organization's culture and guide the behaviors of its employees. Belief systems are an essential component of an organization's control system as they influence how employees perceive and respond to their work environment, their level of engagement and commitment, and their willingness to act in the best interests of the organization.

Belief systems are often reflected in an organization's mission, vision, and values statements, which articulate the company's core beliefs and aspirations. These statements serve as a guide for employees to align their actions with the company's goals and objectives. For example, if a company values innovation and creativity, its belief system may emphasize the importance of experimentation and risk-taking to drive growth and competitiveness.

In addition to mission and values statements, belief systems can also be reinforced through communication channels such as town hall meetings, internal memos, and training programs. By promoting a strong belief system, organizations can create a culture that fosters collaboration, accountability, and a shared sense of purpose, which can improve performance and drive long-term success. Developing belief systems in your organization requires a deliberate and strategic approach.

1. Define your company's mission, vision, and values: These statements should reflect your organization's purpose, aspirations, and core beliefs. They serve as a foundation for developing a strong belief system.

2. Communicate your values: Once you have defined your mission, vision, and values, you need to communicate them to your employees. You can use various channels, such as company meetings, newsletters, or training programs, to reinforce your message and ensure that everyone in the organization understands and supports your beliefs.

3. Lead by example: Your leaders should embody your organization's values and model the behavior you want to see in your employees. This can help reinforce your belief system and create a culture that promotes your values.

4. Encourage employee participation: Involve your employees in the development of your belief system. Encourage them to provide feedback, suggestions, and ideas that align with your organization's mission and values. This can create a sense of ownership and buy-in among your employees.

5. Measure and reinforce: Measure the impact of your belief system on employee engagement, performance, and other relevant metrics. Use this information to reinforce your beliefs and adjust your approach as needed.

Remember that developing belief systems is an ongoing process that requires continuous effort and reinforcement. By creating a strong belief system, you can foster a culture that supports your organization's goals and values, and helps your employees work towards achieving your vision.

The Walt Disney Company, a global media and entertainment conglomerate, has been successful in aligning its strategy over the years by creating a strong belief system. Its strategy framework is built around three pillars: creating high-quality content, utilizing technological innovations, and expanding into new markets. These pillars are rooted in Disney's belief system, which represents the shared values, beliefs, and assumptions that guide the behavior and decision-making of its employees.

Disney's commitment to these pillars can be seen throughout its operations and is reinforced by its belief system. For example, the company's focus on creating high-quality content is driven by its belief in storytelling and its ability to inspire and entertain audiences. This belief is evident in all of Disney's media offerings, from its popular animated movies and TV shows to its theme parks.

Disney's use of technological innovations is also guided by its belief system, which recognizes the importance of staying up to date with the latest trends and technologies. By investing in new technologies such as CGI and VR, Disney is able to enhance its content offerings and provide new and exciting experiences for its audiences.

Furthermore, Disney's expansion into new markets is also aligned with its belief system, which emphasizes the importance of growth and expansion. By acquiring other media and entertainment companies like Pixar, Marvel, and Lucasfilm, Disney is able to expand its content offerings and appeal to an even broader audience while staying true to its core values.

Overall, Disney's focus on these three pillars and its commitment to its belief system have been critical to its success. It has allowed the company to stay relevant and innovative while maintaining a strong brand identity and staying true to its core values.

7

BOUNDARY SYSTEMS

Organizations today have unlimited potential due to advances in technology, globalization, and access to talent and resources from around the world. With the right strategy and execution, companies can rapidly grow and expand their operations, reach new customers and markets, and drive innovation in their industry. However, while the potential for organizations may be unlimited, the time and attention of management is not. Management must balance competing demands for their time, including daily operations, long-term planning, and managing their workforce. They must also stay up to date on the latest trends and technologies, while also ensuring that their organization is meeting its financial goals and maintaining a strong reputation.

To overcome these challenges, organizations need to prioritize their efforts and focus on those areas that will have the greatest impact on their success. This requires a clear understanding of the company's strategic goals and objectives, as well as an ability to prioritize and allocate resources effectively. It also requires a willingness to experiment and take risks, while also maintaining a focus on delivering value to customers and stakeholders.

Boundary systems are the sets of controls that define the limits of acceptable behavior in an organization. They create a framework for decision-making, establish norms for acceptable behavior, and identify consequences for violating those norms. Boundary systems are intended to protect the organization from harm, whether it is reputational damage, legal liability, or financial loss. Examples of boundary systems in organizations include policies and procedures, codes of conduct, and compliance frameworks. These systems define the rules and regulations that employees must follow when conducting business. They also provide guidance on how to handle specific situations, such as conflicts of interest, harassment, or whistle-blowing.

Boundary systems are essential for maintaining order and accountability in organizations. They ensure that employees act in a responsible and ethical manner, and that they are held accountable for their actions. By setting clear boundaries and consequences, boundary systems can help prevent unethical behavior, minimize risk, and promote a culture of compliance and integrity.

It is important to note, boundary systems inform the organization what NOT TO DO. By defining the multitude of opportunities that are out of bounds, they inform the organization whay they SHOULD do. Boundary systems give focus to an organization, which also helps to define the unique value proposition (UVP) of the organization. By clearly defining its UVP, an organization can communicate its distinctive strengths and differentiators that set it apart from competitors.

- Apple: "Think Different." Apple's UVP emphasizes the company's focus on innovation, design, and quality, which sets it apart from competitors in the technology industry.

- Amazon: "Earth's Biggest Selection." Amazon's UVP emphasizes the company's massive selection of products, competitive pricing, and fast delivery, which makes it a convenient and reliable choice for customers.
- Dollar Shave Club: "Shave Time. Shave Money." Dollar Shave Club's UVP emphasizes the company's affordable, high-quality razors, and the convenience of having them delivered directly to customers' doors.
- Tesla: "Accelerating the World's Transition to Sustainable Energy." Tesla's UVP emphasizes the company's focus on innovation, sustainability, and cutting-edge technology, which sets it apart from competitors in the automotive industry.
- Airbnb: "Belong Anywhere." Airbnb's UVP emphasizes the unique experiences and sense of community that travelers can enjoy by staying in local homes and apartments, rather than traditional hotels.

Without established boundaries and guidelines for decision-making and behavior, employees may have conflicting priorities or may be unclear about what is expected of them. This can lead to wasted efforts, lack of management, and ultimately, loss of focus on important initiatives. Additionally, without clear boundaries, there may be a lack of accountability and consistency in decision-making, which can lead to confusion and distrust among employees. There are several types of boundary systems that can be established within an organization to provide guidance and focus for employees.

- Policies and Procedures: These are formal guidelines that outline the specific steps and procedures that employees are expected to follow in various situations. Policies and procedures can cover a wide range of topics, such as human resources, financial management, safety and security, and customer service.
- Codes of Conduct: These are formal statements that outline the organization's expectations for employee behavior, such as ethical behavior, respect for diversity, and compliance with laws and regulations. Codes of conduct can help to create a positive workplace culture and ensure that employees are aligned with the organization's values and mission.
- Performance Metrics: These are quantitative measures that are used to evaluate employee performance and track progress towards organizational goals. Performance metrics can include key performance indicators (KPIs), sales targets, customer satisfaction ratings, and other metrics that are relevant to the organization's strategic objectives.
- Budgets: Budgets are financial plans that allocate resources towards specific initiatives and priorities. By establishing budgets, organizations can ensure that resources are directed towards the most important initiatives and that spending is aligned with the organization's strategic priorities.
- Governance Structures: These are formal structures that define the roles and responsibilities of different stakeholders within the organization, such as board members, executives, and employees. Governance structures can help to ensure accountability and transparency, and provide a framework for decision-

making and communication within the organization.

Overall, these boundary systems can help to provide guidance and focus for employees, and ensure that everyone is aligned with the organization's goals and priorities. By establishing clear boundaries and guidelines, organizations can create a shared understanding of what is expected and what types of behaviors are encouraged, and direct resources towards the most important initiatives.

8

DIAGNOSTIC CONTROL SYSTEMS

D iagnostic control systems are a type of management control system that focuses on identifying and solving problems in a company's operations. They are designed to help managers monitor and analyze the performance of different business processes, identify areas that require improvement, and take corrective actions to ensure that the company achieves its goals.

Diagnostic control systems use various tools and techniques to collect data, analyze it, and provide insights into the performance of different business processes. For example, managers may use key performance indicators (KPIs) to track the progress of different projects or business units, or they may use benchmarking to compare the company's performance to that of its competitors.

In addition to monitoring performance, diagnostic control systems also help managers identify the root causes of problems and take corrective actions to address them. This may involve analyzing the underlying processes that are causing the problems, redesigning those processes, or implementing new procedures to improve performance.

In today's fast-paced and competitive business environment, it is more important than ever for organizations to
monitor and manage their performance against specific targets
and standards. Diagnostic control systems are a key tool in this
process, helping organizations to identify deviations from the
plan and take corrective action to get back on track. From financial controls to quality controls, performance metrics, and
benchmarking, diagnostic control systems provide organizations with the information they need to make data-driven decisions and ensure that they are achieving their strategic
objectives.

- Financial Controls: Financial controls are used to
  monitor and manage financial performance, such as
  revenue, costs, and profits. Financial controls might
  include financial reporting, budgeting, and financial
  analysis.
- Quality Controls: Quality controls are used to
  monitor and manage the quality of products or
  services. Quality controls might include inspections,
  testing, and quality assurance programs.
- Performance Metrics: Performance metrics are used
  to track progress towards specific targets or goals.
  Performance metrics might include key
  performance indicators (KPIs), sales targets,
  customer satisfaction ratings, and other metrics that
  are relevant to the organization's strategic objectives.
- Benchmarking: Benchmarking is the process of
  comparing an organization's performance to that of
  its competitors or industry standards.
  Benchmarking can help organizations to identify
  areas for improvement and best practices that can
  be adopted.

SMART Goals. Defining strategic goals is a primary step in the strategic planning process. Strategic goals are specific, measurable, achievable, relevant, and time-bound (SMART) objectives that support an organization's overall mission and vision. These goals provide direction and focus for the organization, helping to guide decision-making and resource allocation.

KPIs. Once you have defined your strategic goals, identify key performance indicators (KPIs) and metrics that are directly tied to those goals. KPIs and metrics are quantitative measures that help you track progress towards your goals and provide feedback on the effectiveness of your strategies. For example, if one of your strategic goals is to increase customer satisfaction, your KPIs and metrics might include customer satisfaction surveys, Net Promoter Score (NPS), customer retention rates, and repeat purchase rates. These metrics can help you track progress towards your goal and identify areas where you need to make adjustments to your strategy.

Choose KPIs and metrics that are relevant to your goals and that can be tracked and measured over time. By aligning your KPIs and metrics with your strategic goals, you can ensure that you are tracking progress towards your objectives and making data-driven decisions to achieve your mission and vision. Identifying the key areas to focus will help define the critical aspects of the organization that need to be addressed to achieve the strategic goals. The key areas of focus will vary depending on the organization and its goals, but some common areas include:

- Customer satisfaction: This area of focus is essential for any organization as it helps to retain customers and build a strong brand reputation. Customer satisfaction can be measured through surveys, feedback, and reviews.

- Employee engagement: Engaged employees are more likely to be productive and committed to the organization's goals. Employee engagement can be measured through surveys, feedback, and performance reviews.
- Financial performance: Financial performance is critical for the sustainability and growth of the organization. Key metrics to measure financial performance include revenue, profit, and return on investment.
- Operational efficiency: Improving operational efficiency can help the organization reduce costs, improve productivity, and enhance customer satisfaction. Key metrics to measure operational efficiency include cycle time, defect rate, and customer response time.

When brainstorming potential KPIs and metrics, it's important to consider both quantitative and qualitative measures that align with your strategic goals and areas of focus. Quantitative measures are numerical and can be easily tracked and analyzed, while qualitative measures are more subjective and based on feedback and perceptions. By choosing the right KPIs and metrics for each area of focus, you can monitor progress and make data-driven decisions to improve performance and achieve your strategic goals.

Measuring Progress. To effectively measure progress towards strategic goals, organizations must consider the relevance, reliability, and impact of their key performance indicators (KPIs) or metrics. KPIs should be directly related to the organization's key areas of focus and strategic goals to ensure their relevance. Reliability is also crucial, and metrics should be measured accurately and consistently over time, with transparent data and measurement processes. Finally, the impact of

KPIs should be assessed to ensure that they provide meaningful insights and actionable information to improve organizational performance.

Defining targets and thresholds when setting up KPIs and metrics will help to establish clear expectations and a standard for performance. The target is the desired level of performance you want to achieve in a specific KPI or metric, and it should be challenging but achievable. The threshold, on the other hand, is the minimum acceptable level of performance and should be set based on the minimum requirements for achieving your strategic goals.

By defining both targets and thresholds, you can create a clear framework for measuring progress and identifying areas for improvement. This allows you to monitor performance against your goals and make necessary adjustments to your strategy or operations to ensure that you're on track to achieve your desired outcomes.

Assigning Responsibility. Assigning responsibility for tracking each KPI and metric to a specific individual or team ensures accountability and progress monitoring. It helps to identify who is responsible for measuring, analyzing and reporting the data, and who should be taking corrective actions to improve the performance of the metric or KPI. Assigning responsibility also helps to avoid any confusion or ambiguity about who is accountable for the performance of a particular metric or KPI. This can lead to better communication and collaboration between team members, and ultimately better outcomes for the organization.

9

INTERACTIVE CONTROL SYSTEMS

Interactive control systems are a type of management control system that focuses on facilitating communication and collaboration between different levels of an organization. Unlike traditional control systems, which tend to be top-down and hierarchical in nature, interactive control systems are designed to be more collaborative and participative.

Interactive control systems enable managers to share information and collaborate on decision-making in real-time. They allow for open dialogue and discussion between different levels of the organization, which can lead to better decision-making and more effective problem-solving.

One key feature of interactive control systems is that they provide feedback to managers in real-time. This allows managers to make adjustments and take corrective actions as needed, rather than waiting for a periodic performance review.

Another important feature of interactive control systems is that they are adaptable and flexible. They can be adjusted and customized to meet the specific needs of different business units or projects, and they can be modified as conditions change.

- Management by Objectives: Management by Objectives (MBO) is a goal-setting framework that involves setting specific objectives and key results for individuals or teams, and regularly reviewing progress towards those objectives. MBO helps to align individual and team goals with the overall objectives of the organization.
- Performance Appraisals: Performance appraisals are formal evaluations of employee performance, typically conducted on an annual or semi-annual basis. Performance appraisals help to identify areas of strength and weakness and provide feedback for improvement.
- Employee Empowerment: Employee empowerment involves giving employees more autonomy and decision-making authority over their work. Empowering employees can increase motivation and engagement, and help to align individual efforts with the overall goals of the organization.
- Team Meetings: Team meetings are regular meetings between members of a team or department, designed to facilitate communication and collaboration. Team meetings help to align efforts towards shared goals, share information, and identify and address issues and challenges.

Effective communication and collaboration are more important than ever. Interactive control systems are a key tool in this process, helping organizations to facilitate communication and alignment between different levels and functions within the organization. From management by objectives to performance appraisals, employee empowerment, and team meetings, interactive control systems provide organizations with the tools they need to coordinate activities and align efforts towards shared goals.

Designing effective interactive control systems is critical to achieving successful outcomes and optimizing organizational performance. Here are some of the key considerations that are important when designing interactive control systems:

- Clear Goals and Objectives: Interactive control systems should be designed with clear goals and objectives in mind. This means that the system should be aligned with the organization's overall strategy and should be designed to support the achievement of specific business outcomes.
- Appropriate Metrics and KPIs: To ensure that interactive control systems are effective, they must be designed with appropriate metrics and key performance indicators (KPIs). These metrics should be relevant, measurable, and aligned with the organization's goals and objectives.
- Effective Communication and Collaboration: Interactive control systems should be designed to facilitate effective communication and collaboration between different levels of the organization. This includes providing real-time feedback, enabling open dialogue, and encouraging participation from all stakeholders.
- Flexibility and Adaptability: Effective interactive control systems should be flexible and adaptable to changing conditions. This means that the system should be designed to accommodate new data sources, changing business requirements, and evolving organizational needs.
- User-Friendly Interfaces: Interactive control systems should be designed with user-friendly interfaces

that are easy to navigate and understand. This helps to ensure that all stakeholders can use the system effectively and that the insights provided are actionable and meaningful.

The importance of designing effective interactive control systems cannot be overstated. By ensuring that these systems are designed with clear goals, appropriate metrics, effective communication, flexibility, and user-friendly interfaces, organizations can achieve better decision-making, improved problem-solving, and optimized performance.

10

OPPORTUNITIES

The Four Levers of Control framework includes Belief Systems and Interactive Control Systems, both critical components that guide the organization towards opportunities. When designing, these components should be considered as the foundation that outlines "What to do" for the company.

Belief Systems and Interactive Control Systems
inform the organization of what TO DO.

Belief systems are the first lever of control, reflecting the organization's culture, values, and mission. They shape the decision-making processes and define the purpose of the company. Leaders who establish a compelling belief system can align the organization towards a common vision, inspiring employees to work together towards a shared goal.

On the other hand, Interactive Control Systems are the fourth lever of control, emphasizing communication and feedback processes. They enable the organization to learn and adapt while implementing its strategy. These systems promote collaboration, open and honest communication, and identify opportunities for improvement. Effective Interactive Control Systems can create a culture of continuous improvement, helping the organization to respond promptly to changes in the marketplace and seize new opportunities.

The combination of Belief Systems and Interactive Control Systems provides a powerful leadership tool to achieve the organization's objectives. By establishing a clear belief system and Interactive Control Systems, leaders can maintain the organization's focus on its mission and respond quickly to changes in the environment. Additionally, these components promote employee engagement and alignment with the company's goals, resulting in increased productivity, innovation, and job satisfaction.

The integration of Belief Systems and Interactive Control Systems is essential for the long-term success of an organization. Leaders who establish a compelling belief system and effective Interactive Control Systems can create a company that is adaptable, engaged, and focused on achieving its goals and objectives over the long term.

11

FOCUS

The second lever of control, Boundary Systems, assists in establishing rules and guidelines that outline acceptable behavior and actions within an organization. These boundaries define the organization's Unique Value Proposition by clearly stating the thousands of things it will NOT do, promoting discipline and focus.

Boundary Systems and Diagnostic Control Systems inform the organization of what NOT TO DO.

When implemented correctly, Boundary Systems can ensure the organization operates within legal and ethical boundaries, minimizing the risk of non-compliance or unethical behavior. Clear guidelines for decision-making can also ensure consistency and fairness, promoting a culture of trust and respect.

The third lever of control, Diagnostic Control Systems, enables leaders to monitor and evaluate the organization's performance. This includes measurable tasks, milestones, and KPIs. Like boundary systems, by defining what tasks and KPIs to monitor, Diagnostic Controls inform the organization what NOT to do. Developing metrics that align with the overall strategy can help leaders better understand performance and identify areas for improvement. Data-driven decisions based on this information can lead to more effective resource allocation and increased efficiency.

Boundary Systems and Diagnostic Control Systems combined, can ensure that the organization focuses on achieving its goals and objectives. Clear guidelines and monitoring performance against these goals promote employee engagement and motivation, resulting in higher productivity and better outcomes. Leaders can also identify potential risks and issues early on by establishing clear guidelines for decision-making and performance monitoring, taking corrective action before the situation escalates.

Implementing effective Boundary Systems and Diagnostic Control Systems can add significant value to an organization. Promoting focus, consistency, fairness, and data-driven decision-making, leaders can create an organization that is aligned, adaptable, and focused on achieving its goals and objectives over the long term.

PART III

BUILDING A CULTURE OF EXECUTION

Richard Branson is a British entrepreneur, investor, and philanthropist who is best known as the founder of the Virgin Group, a conglomerate of companies that includes Virgin Atlantic Airways, Virgin Records, and Virgin Mobile, among others. He was born on July 18, 1950, in Surrey, England.

Branson started his entrepreneurial journey at a young age, starting with a student magazine and a mail-order record business. He then went on to launch Virgin Records, which became one of the largest independent record labels in the world, with successful acts such as the Sex Pistols and Culture Club.

Over the years, Branson expanded his business empire to include Virgin Atlantic Airways, a leading airline that transformed the aviation industry with its innovative business model and focus on customer experience. He also founded Virgin Mobile, Virgin Galactic, and Virgin Hotels, among other ventures.

Aside from his business activities, Branson is also known for his philanthropic efforts. He founded the Virgin Unite charity organization, which focuses on social and environmental issues. He has also been involved in various environmental campaigns, such as reducing carbon emissions and promoting renewable energy.

Branson is often admired for his adventurous spirit, as he has undertaken various high-profile stunts and record-breaking attempts, including attempting to circumnavigate the globe in a hot air balloon. He has also authored several books, including his autobiography "Losing My Virginity" and "Screw Business as Usual."

Focus on Employees

Richard Branson's approach to employee well-being is deeply rooted in his belief that happy and motivated employees are critical to the success of a business. He recognizes that when employees feel valued, respected, and supported, they are more likely to be engaged, productive, and loyal. Here are some of the ways Branson creates an environment that prioritizes employee well-being:

- Employee empowerment: Branson believes that employees should have a sense of ownership and control over their work. He encourages them to be proactive and to take initiative, and he gives them the autonomy to make decisions and solve problems.
- Open communication: Branson fosters an environment where open communication is encouraged. He regularly communicates with employees, listens to their feedback and ideas, and takes their opinions into consideration when making decisions.
- Work-life balance: Branson recognizes that work-life balance is critical to employee well-being. He

encourages employees to take time off when needed, to prioritize their health and family life, and to take breaks to recharge.

- Recognition and rewards: Branson believes that recognizing and rewarding employees for their hard work is essential. He celebrates successes, acknowledges achievements, and provides incentives for exceptional performance.
- Career development: Branson recognizes that employees want opportunities to grow and develop in their careers. He provides opportunities for training and development, and he encourages employees to take on new challenges and roles within the company.

Overall, Branson's approach to employee well-being reflects his belief that employees are a company's greatest asset. He creates an environment that prioritizes their needs, values their contributions, and fosters a sense of belonging and fulfillment. This approach has helped to create a highly engaged and motivated workforce, which has contributed to the success of his companies.

Open and Flat Organizational Structure

Branson believes in a flat organizational structure where there is less hierarchy and more openness, communication, and collaboration among employees. This means that the traditional top-down management structure is replaced with a more horizontal one, where employees are encouraged to share their ideas and opinions freely, and there are open communication channels for feedback, suggestions, and discussion.

In a flat organizational structure, there are fewer layers of management, which means that decision-making can be faster and more efficient. Instead of having to go through multiple levels of management to get approval for an idea, employees are empowered to make decisions and take action on their own. This approach allows for greater flexibility and agility in responding to changes and challenges.

Branson believes that everyone should have a voice, regardless of their position in the company. He believes that every employee has valuable insights, ideas, and experiences that can contribute to the success of the company. By creating an environment where all employees feel comfortable sharing their thoughts and opinions, he is able to tap into the collective knowledge and creativity of the entire organization.

Additionally, Branson's flat organizational structure promotes a culture of collaboration and teamwork. Because there is less hierarchy and more openness, employees are encouraged to work together to solve problems and make decisions. This approach fosters a sense of shared ownership and accountability, which can lead to greater engagement and commitment to the company's mission and goals.

Overall, the promotion of a flat organizational structure with open communication channels and encouragement of ideas and opinions from all employees reflects his belief in the power of collaboration, empowerment, and inclusivity. This approach has been successful in his companies and has helped to drive innovation and growth.

Emphasis on Innovation

Richard Branson is known for encouraging creativity and innovation in his teams. He recognizes that in today's fast-paced business environment, companies must continuously adapt and innovate to stay ahead of the competition. Branson believes that innovation is not just about developing new products or services, but also about finding new and better ways to operate and serve customers.

Branson's approach to innovation is built on the premise that everyone can contribute to the process, regardless of their role or position in the company. He encourages his teams to think outside the box and to challenge the status quo. He believes that by doing things differently, companies can create a competitive advantage and drive growth.

One way that Branson promotes creativity and innovation is by creating a culture that values experimentation and risk-taking. He believes that failure is an essential part of the innovation process and encourages his teams to take risks and learn from their mistakes. Branson is also known for his willingness to try new things himself, which sets an example for his teams.

Another way that Branson fosters innovation is by providing his teams with the resources and support they need to experiment and explore new ideas. This includes providing funding for research and development, encouraging cross-functional collaboration, and providing training and development opportunities to help employees develop new skills and knowledge.

Finally, Branson believes that innovation is not just about developing new ideas but also about implementing them successfully. He emphasizes the importance of execution and encourages his teams to be persistent and resilient in the face of challenges.

Customer-centric Approach

Branson has always emphasized the importance of putting customers first in his businesses. He believes that providing an exceptional customer experience is the key to building long-term relationships and creating loyal customers.

Branson's focus on the customer experience is reflected in the way his companies operate. He believes that every interaction with a customer is an opportunity to build trust, create a positive impression, and ultimately, drive customer loyalty. Branson understands that customers today have high expectations when it comes to service, and he believes that by exceeding those expectations, his companies can differentiate themselves from the competition.

One way that Branson promotes a customer-centric culture is by empowering his employees to make decisions that benefit the customer. He encourages his teams to listen to customers, anticipate their needs, and take action to resolve issues quickly and efficiently. By giving employees the authority to make decisions on the spot, Branson ensures that his companies are able to respond quickly to customer needs and deliver a high level of service.

Another way that Branson prioritizes the customer experience is by constantly looking for ways to improve. He recognizes that customer needs and preferences are constantly evolving, and he encourages his teams to be proactive in identifying new ways to meet those needs. This includes investing in new technology, training and development programs for employees, and regular customer feedback mechanisms to ensure that his companies are meeting and exceeding customer expectations.

Finally, Branson understands that a great customer experience is about more than just the product or service. He believes that every touchpoint with a customer, from the website to the physical store, should be carefully designed to create a seamless and enjoyable experience. This means paying attention to details like store layout, lighting, and music, as well as ensuring that the product or service itself meets the highest standards of quality.

Embrace of Risk-taking

Richard Branson is known for his willingness to take risks and his belief that calculated risks are necessary for innovation and growth. He understands that taking risks involves the possibility of failure, but he also recognizes that the rewards can be significant if the risks pay off.

Branson encourages his teams to take calculated risks and to be willing to try new things. He believes that by taking risks, companies can create a competitive advantage and drive growth. He also believes that taking risks is essential for innovation, as it allows companies to experiment and explore new ideas.

To promote a culture of risk-taking, Branson fosters an environment that encourages creativity and experimentation. He believes that by providing his teams with the freedom to explore new ideas, they are more likely to take risks and find new ways to innovate. Branson is also known for his willingness to invest in new and untested business ideas, even if they are not yet proven.

Despite his emphasis on risk-taking, Branson also recognizes the importance of managing risk. He encourages his teams to take calculated risks, meaning that they carefully consider the potential rewards and risks before making a decision. He also emphasizes the importance of having a plan in place to manage potential risks and to mitigate any negative outcomes.

Branson and the Four Levers

Richard Branson's management style emphasizes a strong culture of employee empowerment, customer-centricity, innovation, and risk-taking. While this approach has been successful for Branson's businesses, it is important to evaluate its effectiveness through a structured framework. The Four Levers of Control framework is a useful tool for evaluating the success of a business strategy. It examines how a company balances the four levers of control: beliefs systems, boundary systems, diagnostic control systems, and interactive control systems. Using this framework, we can analyze how Branson's management approach has led to the success of his companies, and determine whether this approach can be replicated in other businesses.

Belief Systems

The first lever of control, Belief Systems, involves setting and communicating a clear vision, mission, and set of values that guide decision-making and behavior within an organization. Richard Branson's management approach places a strong emphasis on this lever by prioritizing employee well-being, customer satisfaction, and innovation. He sets a clear vision and values that align with these priorities, and communicates them throughout the organization.

For example, Branson's companies have a strong focus on customer experience and satisfaction. Virgin Airlines, for instance, has a vision to be the world's most loved airline, which is communicated to employees and customers through branding and marketing efforts. This clear belief system is reflected in the way Virgin Airlines provides high-quality in-flight experiences, such as comfortable seating, friendly and attentive staff, and unique offerings like on-board bars and lounges.

Similarly, Branson's emphasis on employee well-being is reflected in his belief system. He recognizes the importance of happy and motivated employees and has established a company culture that prioritizes their well-being. This includes providing flexible working hours, generous vacation time, and other benefits to ensure that employees feel valued and supported.

By setting and communicating clear beliefs, Branson ensures that everyone in the organization understands the priorities and values that guide decision-making and behavior. This helps to create a unified and focused culture that is aligned with the organization's goals and objectives. Ultimately, this lever of control helps to reinforce the company's overall strategy and supports the success of the business.

Boundary Systems

The second lever of control, Boundary Systems, involves creating rules and processes that guide behavior and limit the potential for negative outcomes within an organization. Although Richard Branson's management approach emphasizes risk-taking and creativity, he still recognizes the importance of establishing boundaries to ensure that his companies operate ethically and responsibly.

Branson's companies have policies and procedures in place to protect customer privacy, safety, and security. For example, Virgin Atlantic has a clear set of safety procedures for in-flight emergencies and security measures for airport check-ins. Similarly, Virgin Hotels has strict policies around guest privacy and security.

Another example of Branson's boundary systems is his company's emphasis on ethical business practices. Virgin has a code of conduct that outlines expectations for employee behavior and prohibits unethical practices such as discrimination, harassment, and bribery. This ensures that employees understand the company's expectations for ethical behavior and establishes clear boundaries around acceptable conduct.

By implementing effective boundary systems, Branson ensures that his companies operate ethically and responsibly while still encouraging creativity and risk-taking. This supports the overall success of the business by minimizing the potential for negative outcomes and ensuring that the company's values are upheld.

Diagnostic Control Systems

The third lever of control, Diagnostic Control Systems, involves monitoring performance and providing feedback to ensure that goals are met within an organization. Richard Branson's management approach aligns with this lever as he encourages open communication and transparency within his companies. He believes that by setting clear goals and metrics, companies can track their performance and make adjustments as needed to achieve their objectives.

Branson's companies use metrics and key performance indicators (KPIs) to track performance and provide feedback to employees. For example, Virgin Atlantic tracks its on-time performance, customer satisfaction ratings, and employee engagement levels. This data is regularly shared with employees to keep them informed of their performance and provide feedback on areas where improvements can be made.

In addition, Branson promotes open communication and transparency, which allows for effective diagnostic control systems. He encourages employees to share their ideas and feedback, and he takes the time to listen and respond to their concerns. This allows the company to identify areas for improvement and make necessary adjustments to improve performance.

By using diagnostic control systems, Branson's companies can track their progress towards goals and make necessary adjustments to achieve them. This supports the overall success of the business by ensuring that performance is consistently monitored and optimized to meet organizational objectives.

Interactive Control Systems

The fourth lever of control, Interactive Control Systems, involves fostering collaboration and learning to ensure that the organization adapts and evolves over time. Richard Branson's management approach aligns with this lever as he encourages innovation and collaboration within his companies. He believes that by promoting a culture of continuous improvement, companies can stay ahead of the competition and adapt to changing market conditions.

Branson's companies regularly seek feedback from employees, customers, and stakeholders and use this feedback to improve processes and products. For example, Virgin Mobile regularly conducts surveys to gather customer feedback and uses this feedback to improve its products and services. Similarly, Virgin Hotels uses guest feedback to make improvements to its properties and services.

In addition, Branson encourages collaboration and teamwork within his companies. He believes that by fostering an environment where employees can share their ideas and work together, companies can come up with innovative solutions to business challenges. For example, Virgin Galactic, Branson's space tourism company, has a team of engineers and scientists who collaborate on the development of new technologies and products.

By using interactive control systems, Branson's companies can adapt and evolve over time to meet changing market conditions and customer needs. This supports the overall success of the business by ensuring that the organization is responsive to external factors and continuously improving its products and services.

~

As you read about Branson's successes and the way he has implemented his ideas, take a moment to reflect on your own organization's strategy.

Do you see any similarities between Branson's strategy and your own? Perhaps you both emphasize a customer-centric approach or prioritize innovation and creativity. Or maybe you both value a company culture that fosters collaboration and experimentation.

On the other hand, what are the differences between your strategy and Branson's? Are there areas where your organization could learn from Branson's approach and adopt similar practices? Or do you feel that your organization's strategy is fundamentally different from Branson's and that a different approach would be more effective?

Consider which aspects of Branson's strategy would work well in your organization. Would it be beneficial to adopt his risk-taking mentality, or could you incorporate some of his branding and marketing techniques? Maybe you can leverage his approach to building a diverse and inclusive workforce, or adopt his emphasis on social responsibility.

It's essential to learn from successful business leaders like Richard Branson, but it's also important to remember that every organization is unique. What works for one company may not work for another, so it's crucial to adapt and customize your strategy to fit your organization's needs and goals.

As you ponder Branson's strategy, consider how you can apply his approach to your own organization, and how you can develop a strategy that will lead to success for your company.

12

CREATING THE CULTURE

A company culture refers to the shared values, attitudes, beliefs, behaviors, and practices that characterize an organization. It is the personality of a company and includes the company's mission, vision, ethics, working style, and expectations of its employees. Company culture reflects the company's values, identity, and reputation, and it can have a significant impact on employee morale, productivity, and the overall success of the organization. A strong, positive company culture can attract and retain top talent, while a negative or toxic culture can drive employees away and harm the company's reputation.

- Leading by example: Leaders should model the behaviors and attitudes they want to see in their employees. This means consistently demonstrating the values and priorities of the company, even when faced with difficult decisions or challenging situations.
- Communicating effectively: Leaders need to communicate the company's mission, vision, and

values in a clear and compelling way. They should regularly communicate these messages through a variety of channels, such as company meetings, emails, and internal communications.

- Providing training and development: Leaders should provide opportunities for employees to develop the skills and knowledge needed to succeed in their roles. This includes both job-specific training and development opportunities that support personal and professional growth.
- Celebrating successes: Leaders should celebrate successes and recognize employees who embody the company's values and contribute to its success. This can help reinforce the desired behaviors and create a sense of shared purpose and community within the organization.
- Holding people accountable: Leaders should hold themselves and others accountable for living up to the company's values and executing the strategy. This means setting clear expectations, providing regular feedback, and addressing performance issues promptly and directly.

A culture that supports strategy execution is one where the organization's values, behaviors, and norms align with the strategic direction of the business. In other words, the company's culture supports the implementation of its strategy by promoting the necessary actions and behaviors needed to achieve the desired outcomes.

For example, if a company's strategy is to be innovative and adapt quickly to changes in the market, then a culture of experimentation, risk-taking, and collaboration may be necessary. Conversely, if a company's strategy is to provide reliable and consistent service, then a culture of process adherence and attention to detail may be more appropriate.

Leaders can create a culture that supports strategy execution by actively modeling and reinforcing the desired behaviors, promoting open communication and collaboration, providing adequate resources, recognizing and rewarding success, and addressing any misalignments that may arise. By fostering a culture that supports the execution of the company's strategy, leaders can increase the chances of achieving the desired outcomes and ultimately, the success of the business.

- Communicate the strategy: Make sure the entire organization understands the strategy and how it relates to their role. Communication should be ongoing, not a one-time event.
- Empower employees: Give employees the tools, resources, and authority they need to execute the strategy. This may involve providing training and development opportunities, as well as removing obstacles that hinder progress.
- Foster collaboration: Encourage collaboration and teamwork across the organization, so that everyone is working towards the same goal.

Zappos, an online shoe and clothing retailer has a strong culture that is centered around delivering exceptional customer service, which is aligned with their strategy of providing a seamless and personalized online shopping experience. The company's culture is centered around a set of ten core values, which include "Deliver WOW Through Service," "Create Fun and A Little Weirdness," and "Build Open and Honest Relationships With Communication."

One way Zappos creates its company culture is through a highly selective hiring process. The company looks for people who not only have the necessary skills and experience, but who also embody the company's core values. Zappos also emphasizes transparency and communication, with employees encouraged to speak openly and honestly with one another and with leadership (Heathfield, 2021).

To further support their culture, Zappos has created a number of initiatives and programs, including Zappos Insights, which provides consulting and training services to other companies looking to emulate their culture, and Zappos Family Core, which offers a variety of employee benefits and development opportunities. The company also promotes a sense of community and fun through regular events and activities, such as their annual "Zapponian" family picnic and their "Happiness Experience" team-building program. By creating a culture that is aligned with their strategic goals, Zappos has been able to consistently outperform their competitors and maintain their position as a leader in the online retail industry.

13

THE ROLE OF LEADERSHIP

L eadership plays a crucial role in driving a culture of execution within a company. The leaders are responsible for setting the tone and vision for the company and creating a sense of purpose and direction for the organization. They need to articulate the strategy in a clear and compelling way, so that everyone in the organization understands and can align their actions accordingly.

Leaders also need to lead by example and model the behavior they want to see in others. They need to be visible, accessible, and engaged with their teams, providing guidance, support, and feedback as needed. They need to create a sense of accountability and ownership throughout the organization, so that everyone feels responsible for delivering results.

Finally, leaders need to create a supportive and empowering environment that encourages people to take risks, experiment, and learn from failures. They need to foster a culture of continuous improvement and encourage people to share their ideas and feedback, so that the organization can learn and adapt to changing circumstances.

The role of leadership in driving a culture of execution is

critical, as it sets the tone and direction for the organization and provides the guidance, support, and accountability needed to execute the strategy successfully.

- Set a clear direction by communicating the vision and strategy of the organization. This helps to ensure that everyone is working towards a common goal and has a clear understanding of what needs to be done to achieve it.
- Align incentives with the strategy by tying individual and team goals to the strategic objectives. This helps to ensure that people are motivated and focused on the right things.
- Lead by example by demonstrating the behaviors and actions that they want to see from others. This includes things like being accountable, taking ownership, and being proactive.
- Provide resources and support that people need to execute the strategy effectively. This includes things like training, tools, and technology, as well as coaching and mentoring.
- Foster a culture of innovation by encouraging people to experiment, take risks, and learn from failures. This helps to ensure that the organization is constantly improving and adapting to changes in the market and the environment.
- Measure and track progress against the strategy's goals and KPIs. This helps to ensure that people are accountable for their results and that the strategy is being executed effectively.
- Provide feedback and recognition to people who are contributing to the success of the strategy. This helps to reinforce the right behaviors and to

motivate people to continue working towards the strategic goals.

Herb Kelleher, Southwest Airlines. Herb Kelleher was a visionary leader who founded Southwest Airlines in 1967 and transformed the airline industry with his unconventional approach to business. He was not only a successful CEO, but also a charismatic and inspirational figure who embodied the company's culture of putting people first. Under Kelleher's leadership, Southwest Airlines became known for its low fares, high-quality customer service, and fun-loving culture. Kelleher himself was often seen mingling with employees and passengers, and he encouraged his team to have fun and be themselves on the job (Freiberg & Freiberg, 2019).

Kelleher's management philosophy was based on the belief that happy employees lead to happy customers, which in turn leads to business success. He treated his employees like family, and believed that a company's culture is its most valuable asset. He was also not afraid to take risks, and he was known for his innovative approach to problem-solving. He once famously settled a dispute with a competing airline by arm-wrestling the CEO of the rival company. Kelleher's legacy at Southwest Airlines is still felt today, more than a decade after his retirement. The company's culture of putting people first and having fun on the job remains a core part of its identity, and is often cited as a key factor in its continued success.

Steve Jobs, Apple. Steve Jobs is widely regarded as one of the most influential and visionary leaders in modern business history. As the co-founder and CEO of Apple, Jobs played a critical role in transforming the company from a struggling personal computer manufacturer into one of the world's most successful and innovative technology companies (Beheshti, 2018).

Jobs' leadership style was characterized by a relentless focus on design, user experience, and innovation. He was a master at inspiring and motivating his team to think big and push the boundaries of what was possible. He was also known for his attention to detail and his unwavering commitment to quality, often pushing his team to iterate and refine their work until it was perfect.

Under Jobs' leadership, Apple released a string of groundbreaking products, including the iPod, iPhone, and iPad, that revolutionized the way people interact with technology. He also oversaw the development of the iTunes store, which transformed the music industry, and the App Store, which created a new marketplace for software developers.

Jobs' impact on Apple and the tech industry as a whole is undeniable, and his legacy continues to inspire and influence business leaders around the world.

Indra Nooyi, PepsiCo. Indra Nooyi is an exceptional business leader who has made significant contributions to the success of several companies throughout her career. She joined PepsiCo in 1994 and held various senior leadership roles before being named CEO in 2006, a position she held until 2018 (Freeland, 2020).

During her tenure, Nooyi focused on transforming PepsiCo's product portfolio, shifting towards healthier options and diversifying the company's offerings beyond traditional soda and snacks. She implemented a strategy to reduce the company's environmental footprint, and also led efforts to improve diversity and inclusion within the company.

Nooyi also played a significant role in shaping PepsiCo's culture, emphasizing the importance of continuous learning and development, as well as the need for innovation and risk-taking. She encouraged cross-functional collaboration and created programs to develop and retain talent within the company. Under her leadership, PepsiCo was consistently ranked as one of the best companies to work for.

14

DEVELOPING ACCOUNTABILITY

I n any organization, accountability is a crucial aspect of ensuring that goals are achieved, decisions are made responsibly, and outcomes are delivered effectively. At its core, accountability is about taking ownership of one's actions and being answerable for the results they produce. This can be particularly important in a business setting, where clear performance objectives are established and individuals or teams are held responsible for delivering specific outcomes.

In a corporate context, accountability typically refers to the process of establishing and achieving performance goals, and holding individuals or teams accountable for delivering specific outcomes. This ensures that everyone in the organization is striving for shared objectives, and that results are attained in a timely and efficient manner.

Clear expectations are an essential component of effective performance management. It involves communicating the specific goals, targets, and standards that employees are expected to achieve, along with the metrics for success and the quality and quantity of work expected. When expectations are clearly defined, employees can focus their efforts on meeting those expectations, resulting in increased motivation, productivity, and performance.

To establish a high-performing and engaged workforce, it's essential to foster a culture of ownership. This means creating an environment where employees take responsibility for their tasks, make decisions independently, and feel a sense of accountability towards the company's success. Leaders play a crucial role in creating such a culture by empowering employees, providing resources, recognizing and rewarding contributions, and encouraging open communication. In this way, employees are motivated to take ownership of their work, leading to increased productivity, innovation, and job satisfaction.

Having tough conversations is a necessary skill in both personal and professional settings. These conversations are often uncomfortable, but they are essential for addressing issues and resolving conflicts. Providing feedback is a key component of having tough conversations, as it involves giving someone information about their performance or behavior in order to help them improve. In this way, tough conversations can lead to growth and development, both for the individual receiving the feedback and for the organization as a whole.

The act of providing feedback entails giving constructive comments to someone regarding their performance or behavior, typically within a work or personal development setting. The primary aim of feedback is to aid the individual in enhancing their abilities, knowledge, and overall performance.

- Be specific and objective: When providing feedback, focus on the specific behavior or action and avoid making generalizations or assumptions. Use objective language and avoid subjective judgments.

- Be timely: Provide feedback as soon as possible after the behavior or action has occurred, so that it is fresh in the individual's mind.
- Be constructive: Feedback should be given with the intent of helping the individual improve. Avoid using negative language or attacking the person's character.
- Be actionable: Provide specific recommendations or suggestions for how the individual can improve their performance or behavior.
- Be consistent: Provide feedback regularly and consistently, so that it becomes an ongoing part of the individual's development.

Accountability is essential for ensuring that the organization operates effectively and efficiently, and that everyone is working towards a common goal. It helps to identify areas where performance can be improved and enables leaders to take corrective action when necessary. It also promotes a culture of continuous improvement, where individuals and teams are encouraged to learn from their mistakes and use that knowledge to improve their performance.

- Establish regular check-ins: Schedule regular meetings to review progress, discuss challenges, and provide feedback. These check-ins can be daily, weekly, or monthly, depending on the scope and urgency of the project.
- Use key performance indicators (KPIs): KPIs are measurable indicators of performance that can be used to track progress and identify areas for improvement. Choose KPIs that are relevant to the project and provide regular updates to team members.

- Celebrate successes and address failures: Recognize team members for achieving goals and delivering results. If goals are not met, address the issue immediately and work with the team to identify and resolve the problem.
- Hold people accountable for their actions: If team members are not meeting their commitments, hold them accountable for their actions. This may involve disciplinary action or re-assignment of responsibilities.
- Encourage open communication: Create a culture of openness and transparency, where team members feel comfortable discussing challenges and seeking help when needed.

To be an effective leader, it is important to lead by example. This means that leaders must demonstrate the behavior and values expected of their followers, in order to set the right tone for the organization. When leaders lead by example, they earn the respect and trust of their team members, which is crucial for building a strong and effective team. Leading by example involves consistently making the right choices and being accountable for one's actions, which helps to reinforce the organization's values and beliefs.

For instance, a leader who is committed to a culture of excellence will always strive to do their best, work hard, and demand excellence from themselves and those around them. A leader who leads by example is also accountable and transparent, willing to take responsibility for their actions and not afraid to admit when they are wrong.

Leaders who lead by example set the standard for the entire organization and create a culture of trust, honesty, and transparency. When employees see that their leaders are willing to do what they ask of them, it becomes easier for them to follow suit. Leading by example also creates a positive and productive work environment, leading to increased employee engagement and retention.

Accountability is a crucial aspect of leadership and organizational success. It involves taking responsibility for one's actions, setting clear expectations, fostering a culture of ownership, providing feedback, and holding individuals and teams accountable for their commitments. However, it is important to note that accountability starts with ourselves as leaders. We must model the behavior we expect from others and hold ourselves accountable before holding others accountable. When leaders take ownership of their actions and decisions, it sets the tone for the entire organization and creates a culture of accountability. Therefore, accountability starts with self-reflection and self-improvement before we can expect it from others.

PART IV

CREATING A ROADMAP FOR EXECUTION

One example of a company that created a roadmap for execution is Tesla. In 2016, the company released its "Master Plan, Part Deux," which outlined its long-term goals and roadmap for executing those goals. The plan included four main objectives:

- Create stunning solar roofs with seamlessly integrated battery storage
- Expand electric vehicle product line to address all major segments
- Develop a self-driving capability that is 10X safer than manual via massive fleet learning
- Enable your car to make money for you when you aren't using it

The plan also included specific milestones and timelines for achieving each objective, such as launching the Tesla Semi truck in 2017 and launching a compact SUV and pick-up truck in the following years. By creating this roadmap, Tesla was able to communicate its vision and plan to investors, customers, and employees, and execute on its ambitious goals. Overall, Tesla's "Master Plan, Part Deux" has gone quite well. Here are some key achievements that the company has made since releasing the plan in 2016:

- In 2019, Tesla launched its third-generation solar roof tiles, which are designed to look like traditional roof tiles but have integrated solar cells to generate electricity. The company has also continued to improve its home battery storage products, including the Powerwall and Powerpack.
- Tesla has introduced several new vehicles since releasing its master plan, including the Model 3, Model Y, and Cybertruck. The Model 3 has become the best-selling electric car in the world, and the Model Y has also been well-received.
- Tesla has made significant progress on its Autopilot software, which offers advanced driver assistance features and has the potential to become fully autonomous in the future. The company has collected a massive amount of data from its fleet of vehicles, which is used to improve the software and make it safer.
- Tesla has launched its "Tesla Network" ride-sharing platform, which is designed to allow Tesla owners to make money by renting out their vehicles when they're not using them. However, this initiative is still in the early stages and has not yet been widely adopted.

While there have been some challenges and setbacks along the way, overall Tesla's "Master Plan, Part Deux" has helped the company achieve many of its goals and become one of the most valuable automakers in the world.

Tesla and the Four Levers

In the case of Tesla, the company's belief system is grounded in its mission to accelerate the world's transition to sustainable energy. This belief system is evident in the company's focus on developing electric vehicles and renewable energy solutions.

Boundary systems are also an important part of Tesla's strategy. The company has established clear boundaries for employee behavior, such as safety protocols for its manufacturing facilities and guidelines for driver behavior when using its Autopilot software.

Diagnostic control systems are also critical to Tesla's strategy. The company uses a range of quantitative measures to monitor performance, including production targets, sales figures, and customer satisfaction ratings. These measures allow the company to quickly identify and address issues in its operations.

Finally, interactive control systems play an important role in Tesla's strategy. The company is known for its close communication with customers and stakeholders, including through social media channels. This allows the company to get real-time feedback on its products and services and adjust its strategy as needed.

Overall, Tesla's strategy aligns well with the Four Levers of Control framework, as the company has established clear boundaries for employee behavior, uses quantitative measures to monitor performance, and has established effective communication channels with stakeholders.

While Tesla has made significant progress in recent years, there are still several areas where the company could improve.

- Production and Delivery: Tesla has struggled with production and delivery issues in the past, particularly with the launch of the Model 3. The company has made improvements in this area, but there is still room for improvement to ensure that production can keep up with demand and deliveries are made on time.
- Quality Control: Tesla has also faced criticism for quality control issues with its vehicles, such as paint defects and other cosmetic issues. Improving quality control measures could help the company enhance its reputation and customer satisfaction.
- Autopilot Safety: While Tesla's Autopilot software has many advanced features, it has also been involved in several high-profile accidents. Enhancing the safety features of Autopilot and improving driver training and education could help mitigate these risks.
- Diversification of Product Lines: Tesla is primarily known for its electric vehicles and renewable energy products, but the company may benefit from diversifying its product lines. For example, expanding into new markets such as energy storage or home automation could help the company reach new customers and grow its revenue streams.
- Supply Chain Resilience: Tesla has faced supply chain disruptions in the past, including during the COVID-19 pandemic. Developing a more resilient supply chain could help the company mitigate risks and avoid future disruptions.

Tesla's strategy has proven effective in creating success and driving growth for the company. The Four Levers of Control framework analysis shows that the company has established clear boundaries for employee behavior, uses quantitative measures to monitor performance, and has effective communication channels with stakeholders. While Tesla has faced challenges in the past with production and quality control, safety concerns with Autopilot, and supply chain disruptions, the company has shown a commitment to continuous improvement by actively pursuing solutions to these issues. Overall, Tesla's strategy is well set up for execution, and the company's ongoing efforts to improve suggest a bright future ahead for the electric vehicle and renewable energy leader.

As you consider your own organization's strategy, take a moment to compare it to that of Tesla. Does your organization have a clear roadmap for the future? Have long-term goals been defined and communicated effectively to stakeholders? Or is your organization primarily focused on short-term gains? By comparing your organization's strategy to that of Tesla, you can identify areas where your strategy could be improved and develop a more comprehensive plan that leads to long-term success.

15

DEVELOPING A PLAN FOR STRATEGY EXECUTION

While having a well-crafted strategy is essential, developing a comprehensive plan for executing that strategy is equally important. A detailed plan provides a roadmap for the organization, outlining the specific actions, resources, and timelines required to achieve its goals. It also ensures that everyone in the organization is aligned and working towards a common objective.

One benefit of having a well-thought-out plan is the clarity it provides. The plan outlines what needs to be done, how it needs to be done, and when it needs to be done, helping the organization focus on the tasks at hand and avoid distractions. A plan also provides direction and purpose, helping identify goals and the necessary steps to achieve them. This direction helps keep the organization motivated and focused on objectives.

Time management is another crucial aspect of a comprehensive plan. It allows for effective prioritization of tasks and allocation of time to accomplish everything that needs to be done without feeling overwhelmed. Resource management is also vital, whether it's time, money, or personnel. A plan enables informed decisions about resource allocation to achieve objectives.

Finally, a plan provides a framework for decision-making and problem-solving, allowing for flexibility when unexpected challenges arise. It helps identify solutions and adjust the course of action accordingly. In conclusion, a well-developed plan for executing a strategy is critical to achieving organizational goals and objectives.

Companies that do not have an execution plan often struggle to achieve their goals and may even fail to meet their objectives. Without a well-defined and structured plan, there is no clear roadmap for how to achieve success, which can lead to confusion, disorganization, and wasted resources. The lack of an execution plan can also lead to a lack of focus, with team members pursuing different priorities, making it difficult to make progress towards shared objectives. Additionally, without a plan in place, companies may miss out on potential opportunities, fail to identify and mitigate risks, and struggle to adapt to changes in the market or internal environment. In short, without an execution plan, companies are at a higher risk of failure and may struggle to achieve their goals.

1. Define the goal: Start by defining a clear and measurable goal. Your goal should be specific, realistic, and achievable, and it should align with your company's overall strategic objectives.
2. Identify key stakeholders: Identify the key stakeholders involved in achieving the goal. These may include individuals or teams within your organization, external partners, or other relevant parties.
3. Establish metrics and milestones: Develop a set of metrics and milestones that will be used to track

progress and ensure that the goal is being achieved. This will help you stay on track and make any necessary adjustments to your plan along the way.

4. Allocate resources: Determine the resources that will be required to achieve the goal, including people, budget, and technology. Allocate these resources based on the priority of the different tasks involved.

5. Assign responsibilities: Clearly define who is responsible for each task and ensure that everyone understands their role and what is expected of them.

6. Monitor progress: Establish a regular monitoring and reporting process to track progress and identify any issues or roadblocks. This will help you stay on track and make adjustments as needed.

7. Adjust the plan: Review the plan regularly and make adjustments as necessary to ensure that you stay on track and achieve your goals.

High-Level Examples of Execution Plans

Product Launch

- Establish a cross-functional team with clear roles and responsibilities for each member.
- Develop a timeline and project plan to ensure each task is completed on time.
- Identify potential risks and develop a risk mitigation plan.
- Establish performance metrics to track progress and measure success.
- Implement a launch strategy to support the product release.

- Establish a process for customer feedback and iterate based on that feedback.

Marketing Campaign

- Identify the target audience and develop a marketing persona for each segment.
- Develop messaging that resonates with the target audience and aligns with the brand's value proposition.
- Establish a budget and allocate resources accordingly.
- Develop a campaign timeline and assign tasks to team members.
- Set measurable goals and KPIs for the campaign.
- Launch the campaign and measure results against goals.
- Iterate based on results and refine the campaign as needed.

Business Process Improvement

- Map the current process and identify bottlenecks and inefficiencies.
- Develop a project team with representatives from each area impacted by the process.
- Develop a project plan with clear objectives, timelines, and milestones.
- Assign responsibility and accountability for each task and deliverable.
- Set clear and measurable goals for the project.
- Identify potential risks and develop a mitigation plan.

- Implement the new process and measure results against the goals.
- Iterate based on the results and refine the process as needed.

One example of a well-developed execution plan is the plan created by Tesla for its electric vehicles. The company's execution plan includes multiple elements such as research and development, production, sales and marketing, and service and support.

The first step of Tesla's plan was to invest in research and development to continuously improve the technology and design of the electric vehicles. This involves developing new battery technology and advancing autonomous driving capabilities. The second step is to establish a large-scale production facility that can produce electric vehicles at a low cost. Tesla has built several Gigafactories around the world to support this effort.

The third step is to create a strong sales and marketing strategy that educates potential customers about the benefits of electric vehicles and showcases Tesla's products. Finally, the company has a strong focus on providing excellent service and support to its customers, including offering maintenance and repair services, as well as ongoing software updates to improve the functionality of the vehicles.

Each of these steps is supported by specific actions and goals, as well as a clear timeline and budget. The plan is regularly reviewed and updated to ensure that it remains aligned with the company's overall strategy and goals.

With a clear and well-communicated execution plan, employees have a better understanding of what they need to do and what success looks like. An execution plan can also help a business to adapt to changing circumstances and respond to unexpected challenges. By having a solid execution plan in place, a business is more likely to execute its strategy successfully and achieve its desired outcomes.

16

IDENTIFYING AND PRIORITIZING KEY INITIATIVES

I n order to effectively execute a strategy, it is important to identify and prioritize the key initiatives that will drive the organization towards its goals. This involves taking a strategic approach to determine which initiatives are most important, and then allocating resources and effort accordingly.

Identifying and prioritizing key initiatives means determining the most important projects, programs, or tasks that a company needs to undertake to achieve its strategic objectives. It involves analyzing the business environment, assessing the company's strengths and weaknesses, and setting priorities based on the most significant opportunities and threats. The goal is to focus on the initiatives that will have the most significant impact on the company's performance and allocate resources accordingly. This process helps to ensure that the company's efforts are aligned with its goals and objectives, and that it is making the most effective use of its resources to achieve its desired outcomes.

By identifying and prioritizing key initiatives, you can ensure that your team is working on the most important tasks that will help you achieve your strategic goals. This helps to focus resources and efforts where they will have the greatest impact, and ensures that you are executing the strategy in a logical and effective manner. It also helps to ensure that everyone is aligned and working towards the same priorities, which can help to increase efficiency and productivity.

- Review the strategy: The first step is to review the strategy and identify the key goals and objectives that need to be achieved. This will help you to understand the big picture and identify areas of focus.
- Identify potential initiatives: Brainstorm a list of potential initiatives that could help you achieve your goals. This can include new projects, process improvements, or changes in the way you do business.
- Evaluate each initiative: Evaluate each initiative based on its potential impact on the strategy, the resources required, and the potential risks involved. This will help you to determine which initiatives are primary.
- Prioritize the initiatives: Prioritize the initiatives based on their potential impact on the strategy, the resources required, and the level of risk involved. You may want to use a prioritization matrix or other tool to help you rank the initiatives.
- Align the initiatives with the strategy: Once you have prioritized the initiatives, ensure that they align with the overall strategy. This will help to ensure that your efforts are focused on achieving the goals that are most important to the organization.
- Assign responsibilities: Assign clear responsibilities for each initiative, and ensure that each team

member understands their role in achieving the
goals. This will help to ensure that everyone is
working towards the same objectives.

- Develop an action plan: Develop a detailed action
plan for each initiative, including timelines,
milestones, and resource requirements. This will
help to ensure that you have a clear roadmap for
achieving your goals.

Aligning Initiatives with the Strategy

Aligning initiatives with the strategy means ensuring that the
initiatives identified are directly related to achieving the objectives and goals of the organization's overall strategy. Review and
analyze the strategy and break it down into specific objectives
and goals. Once these objectives and goals have been identified,
the organization can then identify the specific initiatives that
are necessary to achieve them.

For example, if the strategy is to increase customer satisfaction, initiatives might include improving customer service,
creating a more user-friendly website, or offering new products
or services. By ensuring that each initiative is aligned with the
overall strategy, the organization can ensure that its efforts are
focused on achieving its strategic objectives. When evaluating
potential impact of initiatives, you need to consider several
factors that could affect their ability to contribute to achieving
your strategic goals.

- Benefits: Identify the potential benefits of each
initiative, such as increased revenue, reduced costs,
improved customer satisfaction, or enhanced
operational efficiency. Consider the size and scope
of each benefit, as well as the likelihood of achieving
it.

- Risks: Evaluate the potential risks associated with each initiative, such as the risk of failure, the risk of negative customer reactions, or the risk of regulatory noncompliance. Consider the potential impact of each risk, as well as the likelihood of it occurring.
- Costs: Evaluate the costs associated with each initiative, including any upfront costs and ongoing expenses. Consider the total cost of ownership, as well as the potential return on investment.
- Timing: Consider the timing of each initiative in relation to your strategic goals and other initiatives. Evaluate whether the initiative can be completed within the desired timeline, and whether it is aligned with other key initiatives.

Feasibility Assessments

Conducting a feasibility assessment involves evaluating whether an initiative is realistic and achievable. This assessment should consider various factors, such as the availability of resources, the technical and operational feasibility of the initiative, and its alignment with the organization's mission and vision. Conducting a feasibility assessment can help you identify any potential barriers or risks associated with each initiative and determine whether it is a viable option for achieving your strategic goals.

- Resources: Determine whether you have the necessary resources, including financial, human, and technological resources, to execute the initiative effectively.
- Technical feasibility: Assess whether the initiative is technically feasible, including any potential

challenges or limitations that may arise during
implementation.

- Operational feasibility: Evaluate whether the
  initiative is operationally feasible, considering
  factors such as the impact on existing processes and
  systems, and the level of organizational change
  required.
- Alignment with mission and vision: Consider
  whether the initiative aligns with the organization's
  mission and vision, and whether it supports the
  organization's long-term goals and objectives.

Prioritization Frameworks

Using a prioritization framework helps you evaluate and rank
each initiative based on its potential impact and feasibility.
There are different types of frameworks you can use, such as
the cost-benefit analysis, the impact-effort matrix, or the risk vs.
reward matrix.

- A cost-benefit analysis involves comparing the
  expected costs of an initiative to the expected
  benefits it will provide. This helps you identify the
  initiatives that will provide the most value for the
  resources invested.
- An impact-effort matrix helps you visualize the
  potential impact and effort required for each
  initiative. By plotting each initiative on a two-
  dimensional grid based on its potential impact and
  the effort required, you can easily identify the
  initiatives that are both high impact and low effort,
  and prioritize them accordingly.
- A risk vs. reward matrix helps you evaluate each
  initiative based on the potential risks and rewards

associated with it. By identifying the potential risks and rewards of each initiative, you can prioritize the initiatives that offer the most potential reward with the lowest level of risk.

Input and Feedback

Seeking input and feedback from key stakeholders is a critical step for identifying and prioritizing key initiatives for executing a strategy. It helps to ensure that you have considered different perspectives and taken into account potential roadblocks or challenges. Seeking input and feedback is a critical step in identifying and prioritizing key initiatives for executing a strategy, and can help to ensure that you are making the most effective use of your resources and efforts.

- Gaining different perspectives: By involving various stakeholders, you can gain different perspectives on the potential impact and feasibility of each initiative. This can help you identify potential risks or opportunities that you may not have considered on your own.
- Building buy-in and support: By involving stakeholders in the process, you can build buy-in and support for the initiatives that are ultimately selected. This can help ensure that the necessary resources and support are available to execute the initiatives effectively.
- Improving decision-making: By seeking input and feedback, you can make more informed decisions based on a wider range of information and perspectives. This can help you identify the most promising initiatives and avoid potential pitfalls.

- Enhancing communication and collaboration: By involving stakeholders in the process, you can enhance communication and collaboration between different teams and departments. This can help to break down silos and improve cross-functional alignment.

By identifying dependencies between initiatives, you can prioritize them in a logical sequence that allows for the most efficient and effective execution of the strategy. You can ensure that initiatives that are dependent on each other are executed in the correct order, and that any necessary resources are allocated accordingly. Additionally, by understanding the dependencies between initiatives, you can anticipate potential roadblocks and develop contingency plans to mitigate any risks.

17

DEFINING ROLES AND
RESPONSIBILITIES

Defining roles and responsibilities involves clearly outlining the specific tasks and activities that each person within a team or organization is responsible for completing in order to achieve the goals and objectives of the company. This includes determining who is responsible for making decisions, who is accountable for specific outcomes, who needs to be consulted or informed, and who is responsible for executing different aspects of the plan. By defining roles and responsibilities, everyone on the team has a clear understanding of their own responsibilities and what they are expected to contribute to the overall success of the initiative. This helps to avoid confusion, duplication of effort, and missed deadlines, and ensures that everyone is working towards the same end goal.

If roles and responsibilities are not clearly defined within an organization, it can lead to confusion, inefficiency, and a lack of accountability. Without clear roles and responsibilities, employees may not know who is responsible for which tasks, leading to duplicated efforts or tasks being left undone. This can result in missed deadlines, poor quality work, and ultimately, a negative impact on the company's bottom line. Additionally, unclear roles and responsibilities can lead to employee dissatisfaction and disengagement, as individuals may feel frustrated by a lack of direction and accountability.

When defining roles, identify the specific responsibilities and tasks associated with each role. This means breaking down the functions and tasks required to execute each initiative into specific roles that individuals or teams will be responsible for. For example, if one of the key initiatives is to improve the customer experience, some of the functions and tasks required may include conducting customer research, analyzing feedback, developing new processes and procedures, and training staff.

To define the roles for this initiative, you would identify the job titles and descriptions that are required, such as a Customer Research Analyst, a Process Improvement Specialist, a Customer Service Trainer, and so on. You would then outline the specific responsibilities and tasks associated with each role, such as conducting surveys, analyzing data, developing training materials, and delivering training sessions.

Identifying dependencies between roles ensures a smooth execution of the strategy. For instance, some tasks may rely on the output of others, so the work of one role must be completed before another can begin. Identifying these dependencies can help to plan and sequence the work effectively and efficiently. Once dependencies have been identified, communicate them to the team so that everyone understands the interdependencies and how their work fits into the larger picture. This can help to ensure that the team is working together effectively and can prevent delays or rework that might occur due to misunderstandings or misaligned work.

Once the roles have been identified and defined, assign

specific responsibilities to each team member. This means that each person knows exactly what they are responsible for, what is expected of them, and what the deadlines are for their tasks.

- Identify key activities: Start by identifying the key activities required to execute the strategy. This may involve breaking down the strategy into specific tasks and actions that need to be taken.
- Determine the skills required: Once you have identified the key activities, determine the skills and capabilities required to complete each task successfully.
- Assign roles: Based on the skills and capabilities required, assign specific roles to team members. Each role should have clear responsibilities, including specific tasks and actions that need to be taken.
- Define reporting lines: Clarify reporting lines and communication channels between team members and with the leadership team. This will ensure that everyone knows who to communicate with and when.
- Establish accountability: Ensure that each team member understands their level of accountability for their role and the tasks assigned to them. This may involve establishing specific KPIs and metrics to measure performance.
- Review and adjust: Regularly review and adjust roles and responsibilities as needed to ensure that they remain aligned with the strategy and the evolving needs of the organization.

Establishing an accountability framework helps keep

everyone on the same page and ensures that progress is being made towards the strategic goals. By regularly reviewing and adjusting the roles and responsibilities, you can ensure that they remain relevant and aligned with the evolving needs of the organization.

PART V

MANAGING EXECUTION

One example of a company that manages execution well is Amazon. The company is known for its "obsessive" focus on customer satisfaction, which drives its strategy and execution. Amazon's execution is driven by a set of core principles, including customer obsession, ownership, bias for action, and a willingness to experiment and learn from failures.

To ensure successful execution of its strategy, Amazon has developed a range of tools and processes, including a strong project management system, data-driven decision-making, and a culture of innovation and continuous improvement. The company also emphasizes speed and agility, and encourages its employees to take calculated risks and make decisions quickly.

Furthermore, Amazon's leadership team sets clear goals and metrics for each business unit, and holds team members accountable for delivering results. The company uses regular performance reviews and feedback mechanisms to help employees stay on track and make course corrections as needed.

Amazon's management and execution practices can be analyzed through the Four Levers of Control framework.

- Belief systems: Amazon's core belief system is centered around customer obsession. This belief drives the company's strategy and execution, with a focus on delivering exceptional customer experiences and meeting their needs.
- Boundary systems: Amazon has established clear boundaries for employee behavior through its leadership principles and code of conduct. These guidelines ensure that all employees understand what is expected of them and how they should conduct themselves to achieve the company's goals.
- Diagnostic control systems: Amazon's performance measurement and monitoring systems are driven by data and analytics. The company uses key performance indicators (KPIs) to measure progress toward strategic goals, and employs a range of analytics tools to track customer behavior, market trends, and other metrics that help inform decision-making.
- Interactive control systems: Amazon's interactive control systems are designed to foster communication, collaboration, and innovation. The company encourages employees to share ideas, experiment with new approaches, and learn from failures. It also uses feedback mechanisms such as performance reviews and coaching to help employees develop their skills and achieve their goals.

Overall, Amazon's management and execution practices align well with the Four Levers of Control framework. The company has a strong belief system centered around customer obsession, clear boundary systems to ensure employee behavior aligns with strategic goals, diagnostic control systems driven by data and analytics, and interactive control systems that foster communication, collaboration, and innovation.

Executing a strategy can be a complex and challenging process, and it is important to evaluate your organization's potential for success in this area. Take a moment to consider the following questions:

Firstly, is there a clear plan in place for executing your organization's strategy? Has this plan been effectively communicated to employees and stakeholders? Is there a timeline in place for achieving key milestones? If there are any gaps in the plan, these should be addressed to ensure that the strategy can be executed successfully.

Secondly, do you have the assets necessary to execute the strategy? This may include financial resources, physical infrastructure, technology, and human capital. Are these assets sufficient to support the execution of the strategy? Are there any gaps that need to be addressed?

Thirdly, is leadership aligned around executing the strategy? Do senior leaders and managers share a common understanding of the strategy and its goals? Are they committed to supporting the execution of the strategy? Without strong leadership support, it may be difficult to successfully execute the strategy.

In addition to these questions, it is also important to consider potential barriers to execution, such as external market conditions, regulatory changes, or disruptions in the supply chain. By evaluating your organization's potential for successfully executing its strategy, you can identify areas where improvements are needed and develop a plan to overcome any obstacles that may arise. This will increase the likelihood of achieving long-term success and growth.

18

TRACKING PROGRESS

Tracking progress is an essential component of effective strategy execution. Without a system in place to measure progress towards goals, it can be difficult to determine if the organization is on track to achieve its objectives.

Tracking progress means regularly measuring and monitoring the status and advancement of an initiative, project or goal. It involves identifying specific metrics or KPIs (Key Performance Indicators) that help to assess whether the initiative is on track and making progress towards achieving its objectives. Tracking progress allows leaders to understand how well their plans are being executed and to identify any issues or areas for improvement. It also enables them to make informed decisions and take corrective actions when necessary. By tracking progress, leaders can gain insights into what is working well and what needs to be improved to achieve the desired outcomes. Defining your company's KPIs requires a thoughtful and structured approach.

- Identify your business goals: Start by identifying your overall business objectives. Then, break them down into specific goals that you want to achieve.
- Determine the metrics: Determine the metrics that you need to track to measure progress towards each goal. Think about which metrics are most relevant to your business and how you can use them to inform your decision-making.
- Set targets: Set specific, measurable targets for each metric. This will help you determine whether you are on track to achieve your goals.
- Assign ownership: Assign responsibility for tracking each KPI to specific individuals or teams within your organization. Make sure they have the necessary resources and support to succeed.
- Establish reporting and review procedures: Establish a regular reporting schedule and review process to ensure that progress is tracked and communicated to relevant stakeholders.
- Continuously evaluate and adjust: Continuously evaluate the effectiveness of your KPIs and adjust them as needed to ensure they remain relevant and aligned with your business goals.

There are many KPIs that can be used in business, and the specific KPIs used will depend on the goals of the business and the industry it operates in.

- Revenue: This KPI measures the amount of money a company is generating in sales. It is a key indicator of the health of the business.
- Gross Profit Margin: This KPI measures the percentage of revenue that is left over after deducting the cost of goods sold. It provides insight

into how efficient a company is at managing its costs.

- Customer Acquisition Cost: This KPI measures how much it costs a company to acquire a new customer. It can help companies understand the effectiveness of their marketing and sales efforts.
- Customer Lifetime Value: This KPI measures the total amount of money a customer is expected to spend on a company's products or services over their lifetime. It can help companies understand the long-term value of their customers.
- Employee Turnover: This KPI measures the percentage of employees who leave a company over a specific period of time. It can help companies understand how satisfied their employees are and identify areas where improvements can be made.
- Net Promoter Score: This KPI measures how likely customers are to recommend a company's products or services to others. It can help companies understand how well they are meeting the needs of their customers and identify areas where improvements can be made.

When designing KPIs, it's important to make sure that they are aligned with the company's overall strategic objectives. This means that the KPIs should be clearly linked to the core mission and vision of the organization, and should help to track progress towards achieving these higher-level goals.

The KPIs should also be SMART (Specific, Measurable, Achievable, Relevant, and Time-bound). Each KPI should be clearly defined with specific targets and milestones that are measurable over time. This will enable the organization to track its progress and make informed decisions about what is working and what needs to be adjusted.

It's also important to identify the right metrics to measure. Not all KPIs are the same for all organizations. Consider a metric used in online companies such as time-on-page (TOP), the amount of time a user spends on each page of a company's website. A news organization such as The Wall Street Journal would want to increase average TOP. They may look to create more enticing headlines or improve their writing to keep customers on each page longer, so they can serve more ads. Whereas a company such as search giant Google builds their reputation on delivering the customer's search results as fast as possible. Google in this case would want to lower the average TOP as much as possible. As you see, KPIs are not the same across all organizations. They need to be aligned with the critical success factors for the individual organization and reflect the core activities that drive value for the business.

19

COMMUNICATING PROGRESS

Effective communication is an essential aspect of successful strategy execution. Once a plan is in place and progress is being tracked, it is important to communicate this progress to stakeholders within and outside the organization. Communicating progress not only keeps everyone informed about the status of initiatives, but it also helps build trust and transparency. This is especially important when unexpected challenges arise or when changes need to be made to the plan.

Effective communication is critical for building and maintaining relationships, managing conflicts, and achieving business goals. In today's fast-paced business environment, communication has become more complex and challenging due to the increased use of technology and the global nature of business.

Clear communication is important for creating a shared understanding of business objectives, strategies, and expectations. When communication is not clear, employees may misunderstand their roles and responsibilities, leading to confusion and errors. Effective communication also helps build trust and credibility with customers and other stakeholders, leading to long-term relationships and repeat business.

In addition to these benefits, communication plays a critical role in managing conflicts within the organization. Conflicts can arise due to differences in opinions, personalities, or goals. When communication channels are open, conflicts can be addressed and resolved before they escalate into more significant issues that can harm the organization's reputation.

Effective communication also helps organizations achieve their business goals by providing timely and relevant information to decision-makers. When decision-makers have access to accurate and timely information, they can make informed decisions that lead to better outcomes.

In any business or organizational setting, there are many individuals or groups that have a vested interest in the success or failure of a project or initiative. These individuals or groups are known as stakeholders, and they can play a critical role in determining the outcome of the project.

Stakeholders are individuals or groups that have an interest in or are affected by the activities and decisions of a business. They can include employees, customers, shareholders, investors, suppliers, government entities, and the community where the business operates. Stakeholders can have a significant impact on a company's success, and it is important for businesses to identify and understand their stakeholders' needs and interests, as well as how their actions may affect those stakeholders. By actively engaging with stakeholders and addressing their concerns, companies can build stronger relationships, improve their reputation, and enhance their long-term viability.

Defining the **Primary Stakeholder** of a company involves identifying the individual or group that is most affected by the decisions, actions, and outcomes of the company. This can be done by considering the impact of the company's activities on different individuals, groups, or entities, and determining which of these stakeholders has the most significant interest or influence on the company.

The primary stakeholder of a company is often the group or individual that has the most significant financial interest in the company's success or failure. This could be the company's investors, shareholders, or owners, whose primary concern is the financial performance of the company and the return on their investment. However, there may be other stakeholders that are also important to consider when defining the primary stakeholder of a company. These may include customers, employees, suppliers, regulatory bodies, and the broader community, each of which may have different interests and concerns that need to be taken into account.

Defining the Primary Stakeholder

Mission statements define the primary stakeholder by stating the company's purpose and who the company is serving. The stakeholder may be the customer, the employee, the owner/shareholder, or a combination of them. The mission statement communicates the company's core values and beliefs, and serves as a guide for decision-making and goal-setting. By identifying the primary stakeholder in the mission statement, the company is making a commitment to prioritize the needs and interests of that stakeholder in all its operations and activities.

A company can have multiple primary stakeholders. In fact, it's common for companies to have multiple stakeholders, such as customers, employees, shareholders, and the community. The key is for the company to prioritize and balance the needs and interests of each stakeholder group in a way that is sustainable and supports the long-term success of the business. This can involve making strategic decisions and trade-offs to ensure that each group's needs are being met and that the company is fulfilling its broader social and ethical responsibilities.

A company's mission statement that puts employees as the primary stakeholder is from the outdoor clothing and gear company Patagonia. Their mission statement reads, "Build the best product, cause no unnecessary harm, use business to inspire and implement solutions to the environmental crisis." This statement highlights the company's commitment to creating high-quality products while also minimizing their environmental impact. It also emphasizes the importance of using business as a force for good, which includes providing fair wages and working conditions for employees. By prioritizing the environment and social responsibility, Patagonia recognizes that their employees are the primary stakeholders.

A mission statement that puts the owners as the primary stakeholder is from the pharmaceutical company Pfizer: "To be the world's premier, most valued pharmaceutical company. To discover, develop, and provide innovative products and services that save and improve lives around the world, while maximizing shareholder value." In this statement, the focus is on maximizing shareholder value, making the owners the primary stakeholder.

A mission statement that puts the customer as the primary stakeholder is seen at Delta Air Lines. "Deliver exceptional customer experiences that drive loyalty and growth." In this mission statement, Delta Air Lines emphasizes the importance of providing exceptional customer experiences that will result in customer loyalty and business growth. By prioritizing the customer as the primary stakeholder, Delta aims to differentiate itself from its competitors and build long-term relationships with its customers.

While a company may have multiple stakeholders, it is crucial to identify and prioritize the primary stakeholder, as they are the ones who have the most significant impact on the success of the company. Therefore, companies need to ensure that their mission statements reflect the needs of their primary stakeholder and communicate progress towards meeting their expectations. By doing so, companies can build a strong foundation for sustainable growth and long-term success.

20

MAKING COURSE CORRECTIONS

Even the best-laid plans can go awry, and it is crucial to be able to identify when things are not going as planned and make the necessary adjustments. Companies may need to make a course correction when they realize that they are not on track to achieve their goals or when external circumstances change. For example, if a company has set a goal to increase sales by a certain amount in a given period but finds that they are falling behind schedule, they may need to make a course correction to realign their efforts and resources with their target. Similarly, if an external factor such as a change in the regulatory environment or a global pandemic affects a company's operations, they may need to make a course correction to adapt to the new circumstances.

In business, course correction refers to the act of adjusting or changing an organization's plans, strategies, or actions when its goals are not being met or when there is a deviation from the intended path. Course correction is important because it allows companies to respond to changing market conditions, unexpected events, or errors in execution, and ultimately helps them achieve their objectives.

To make a course correction, companies must first identify the root cause of the problem or deviation. This requires a systematic approach of analyzing data, reviewing feedback from customers and stakeholders, and evaluating internal processes and resources. Once the cause is identified, the company can determine the most effective course of action to address it. This may involve adjusting the strategy, reallocating resources, or redefining roles and responsibilities.

In 2011, Netflix, a company that offered DVD rental-by-mail and online streaming services, made a strategic decision to split their business into two separate entities: one for DVD rentals and another for streaming (Richwine & Adegoke, 2011). However, this decision turned out to be a course correction that was necessary for the company. Despite their success at the time, the decision to split the business resulted in losing 800,000 subscribers in a single quarter and a significant drop in the company's stock price. The move angered customers who were accustomed to having access to both services for one price.

After facing a significant setback in the form of lost subscribers and a falling stock price, Netflix responded to the situation by taking corrective action. They realized that their decision to split the business had caused a backlash from their customers and decided to reverse the decision. By refocusing their efforts on their online streaming service, they demonstrated their commitment to meeting the needs of their primary stakeholders, the customers. Additionally, the company took steps to regain customer trust by improving the user interface and expanding their content library. By prioritizing their customers' satisfaction, Netflix was able to recover from the damage and reposition themselves as a leader in the industry. This example highlights the importance of making course corrections when necessary and prioritizing the needs of primary stakeholders in order to achieve long-term success.

By contrast, Blockbuster's failure to make a course correction when it was necessary ultimately led to the company's downfall. Their inability to recognize and adapt to changing market trends and technology was a critical misstep that allowed their competitors to gain an edge. By not introducing an online rental service and subscription model earlier, Blockbuster lost out on a significant portion of the market to companies like Netflix. The failure to make a course correction and adjust their business model proved to be a fatal mistake, and the company ultimately filed for bankruptcy in 2010. This serves as a cautionary tale for businesses to remain vigilant and adaptive in their approach to remain competitive in an ever-changing market.

It is important for companies to be agile and adaptable in making course corrections. This requires a culture of openness to change, where feedback and ideas are welcomed from employees at all levels. It also requires a willingness to take calculated risks and a commitment to continuous improvement. By making course corrections, companies can better meet the needs of their stakeholders and improve their overall performance.

PART VI

OVERCOMING EXECUTION CHALLENGES

Any discussion about overcoming challenges would not be complete without talking about Apple. As of 2021, Apple is considered the second most valuable brand in the world at $263.4 billion, second only to Amazon's value of $334.6 billion. So why do we think of Apple when discussing overcoming challenges? That is because a mere 25 years ago, Apple was a failing company on the verge of bankruptcy.

Using the Four Levers of Control framework, deep seated issues can be found across all levers.

Diagnostic Control Systems: Apple's diagnostic control systems were failing to provide accurate feedback on the company's performance for several reasons. Firstly, the company had a fragmented product line that was confusing to customers. Apple was trying to cater to too many market segments at once, which resulted in a lack of focus and clarity. This made it difficult for the company to accurately measure the performance of its products and make data-driven decisions to optimize its product line.

Secondly, Apple was struggling to innovate, and its product

line had become stagnant. The company had failed to keep up with the changing market dynamics and the emergence of new technologies, which resulted in a lack of differentiation and competitive advantage. This made it difficult for Apple to accurately measure its performance against competitors and identify areas for improvement.

These issues were compounded by the lack of clear diagnostic control systems in place at Apple. The company lacked a clear and consistent approach to measuring its performance across its product line, and the feedback it received was often incomplete or inaccurate. This made it difficult for Apple to identify the root causes of its problems and take corrective action to address them.

Belief Systems: Apple's belief systems were not aligned with the company's goals, which was a significant challenge for the company in the mid-1990s. The company had lost its focus on innovation, which was one of the core values that had driven its success in the early years. Instead, Apple had become too focused on the development of too many products to cater to too many market segments simultaneously.

This lack of focus on innovation was a significant departure from Apple's original vision, which was to create innovative products that changed the way people interacted with technology. By shifting its focus away from innovation and towards a more product-centric approach, Apple had lost sight of its core strengths and competitive advantages.

Furthermore, the company's approach to developing products for too many market segments simultaneously was misguided. By trying to cater to everyone, Apple risked becoming a "jack of all trades, master of none." This approach resulted in a fragmented product line that was confusing to customers and made it difficult for the company to differentiate itself from its competitors.

Boundary Systems: In the case of Apple in the 1990s, the company lacked clear boundary systems, which contributed to a fragmented product line, a lack of focus, and confusion among customers.

One of the main problems was that Apple was trying to cater to too many market segments at once, resulting in a product line that was confusing and difficult to navigate for customers. This lack of focus and clarity was partly due to the absence of clear boundary systems that would have limited the number of products that Apple could develop and bring to market.

The absence of clear boundary systems also meant that there was no clear roadmap for product development or a clear understanding of what constituted a successful product. This led to a lack of coherence in the product line, with products that were not aligned with the company's goals or that failed to resonate with customers.

Furthermore, the lack of clear boundary systems meant that there was no clear accountability or responsibility for the development and success of products. This led to a lack of ownership among employees and a lack of commitment to the company's goals and objectives.

Interactive Control Systems: Interactive control systems refer to the mechanisms that enable organizations to continuously monitor and adjust their performance in response to changing circumstances. In the case of Apple, there was a lack of interactive control systems, which contributed to a lack of feedback on the company's performance and a failure to make timely adjustments to strategy and operations.

One of the key problems was that Apple's management lacked a clear understanding of the changing market dynamics and the emergence of new technologies. As a result, the company failed to anticipate changes in customer preferences and market trends, and it was slow to react to these changes.

Another issue was that Apple's feedback mechanisms were

not effective in providing accurate and timely information about the company's performance. The company lacked a consistent approach to measuring performance across its product lines, and the feedback it received was often incomplete or inaccurate. This made it difficult for Apple to identify the root causes of its problems and take corrective action to address them.

Finally, Apple's management lacked the tools and resources necessary to make timely adjustments to strategy and operations. The absence of interactive control systems meant that there was no clear mechanism for communicating performance information to decision-makers or for making rapid adjustments to operations based on that information.

∼

Apple was in dire straits in the mid-1990s and needed a radical overhaul to survive. It was losing market share, had no clear vision for the future, and was facing stiff competition from its rivals. To overcome these challenges, Apple implemented several key changes in its strategy and execution.

Rebuilding the Leadership Team

In the late 1990s, Apple's board of directors brought back Steve Jobs as CEO in 1997. Jobs, who had co-founded Apple in the 1970s and was known for his innovative ideas and vision, set about restructuring the company's leadership team and setting a new direction for the company.

One of the first things Jobs did was to consolidate Apple's product lines and focus on a few key products that could drive growth and innovation. This included the iMac, which was designed to be a more user-friendly and aesthetically pleasing desktop computer, and the iPod, which revolutionized the music industry by allowing users to carry thousands of songs in their pocket.

Jobs also introduced a new design philosophy that focused on simplicity and elegance, which became a hallmark of Apple's products. He also insisted on tight control over the design and manufacturing process, which helped to improve product quality and consistency.

In addition to these changes, Jobs also made key hires to the company's leadership team, including Tim Cook as the Chief Operating Officer (COO). Cook was tasked with improving Apple's supply chain management and manufacturing processes, which helped to ensure that products were produced efficiently and delivered on time.

Streamlining Product Lines

Steve Jobs decided to streamline Apple's product lines and focus on a few key products that could drive growth and innovation. One of the first products that Apple focused on was the iPod, which was introduced in 2001. The iPod was a revolutionary product that allowed users to carry thousands of songs in their pocket, and it quickly became a cultural phenomenon. The iPod was not only a music player but a platform for Apple to showcase its innovative design and user experience capabilities. The success of the iPod allowed Apple to reposition itself as a consumer electronics company and established its reputation for innovative products.

Building on the success of the iPod, Apple later introduced the iPhone in 2007. The iPhone was a revolutionary product that transformed the mobile phone market. It combined a mobile phone, music player, and internet browser into one device and set a new standard for mobile user experience. The iPhone's innovative design and features helped to drive Apple's growth and establish its reputation as a technology innovator.

By focusing on a few key products, Apple was able to streamline its operations and invest more resources in research and development, which led to the development of even more innovative products. Apple's focus on innovation and user experience design set it apart from its competitors.

Investing in Research and Development

Under the leadership of Steve Jobs, the company was known for its relentless focus on design and user experience, which often required significant R&D investment to develop new technologies and designs that set it apart in the market.

One example of Apple's investment in R&D is the development of the iPhone. The iPhone required significant R&D investment to develop new hardware and software technologies, including the multi-touch screen, mobile operating system, and mobile processor. This investment paid off with the launch of the iPhone in 2007, which quickly became a cultural phenomenon and transformed the mobile phone market.

Apple has also invested in R&D to develop new products and technologies in other areas, such as the Apple Watch and AirPods. The development required significant R&D investment to develop new technologies such as miniaturized sensors and custom chips.

Another area where Apple has invested in R&D is in renewable energy and sustainability. Apple has committed to achieving 100% renewable energy use in all of its facilities and has invested in renewable energy projects such as solar and wind power. Apple has also developed new materials and manufacturing processes that reduce the environmental impact of its products.

By investing in R&D, Apple has been able to stay ahead of competitors and maintain its position as one of the most valuable and influential companies in the world.

Improving Supply Chain Management

Under the leadership of Tim Cook, who was previously the company's Chief Operating Officer and was responsible for managing Apple's global supply chain, the company has developed one of the most efficient and effective supply chains in the world.

Apple works closely with its suppliers and manufacturers to ensure that products are produced efficiently and delivered on time. This requires a high level of collaboration and coordination across a complex network of suppliers and manufacturers located all over the world. Apple has developed strong relationships with its suppliers and manufacturers and has implemented a range of best practices and processes to ensure that products are produced to the highest quality standards and delivered on time.

One key aspect of Apple's supply chain management is its use of just-in-time (JIT) inventory management. This involves closely coordinating production schedules with supplier deliveries to ensure that inventory is minimized and products are delivered to customers as quickly as possible. Apple's focus on just-in-time inventory management has helped to minimize inventory costs and improve efficiency throughout the supply chain.

Apple has also invested in advanced manufacturing technologies and processes, such as robotics and automation, to improve the efficiency and quality of its production processes. By using these technologies, Apple has been able to streamline production, reduce costs, and improve the quality and consistency of its products.

∽

Steve Jobs' leadership style and strategic decisions helped Apple regain its position as one of the most innovative and successful companies in the world. Using the Four Levers framework, we can see how Jobs turned the company into the success it is today.

Belief Systems: Jobs believed that Apple should be a company that challenged the status quo, pushed the boundaries of innovation, and created products that people didn't even know they needed. He believed in design, simplicity, and ease-of-use, and instilled these values into the company's culture. He also believed in focusing on a few key products and making them exceptional. He famously said, "People don't know what they want until you show it to them."

Boundary Systems: Jobs used boundary systems to create a sense of discipline and accountability within Apple. He eliminated many of the product lines that were dragging the company down, and he set strict deadlines for product development. He also established a culture of secrecy and control around product launches, which helped build anticipation and excitement among Apple's customers.

Diagnostic Control Systems: Jobs used diagnostic control systems to keep a close eye on Apple's financial performance and product development. He was known for his attention to detail and his ability to spot problems before they became serious. He also used customer feedback to make improvements to Apple's products and services.

Interactive Control Systems: Jobs used interactive control systems to foster collaboration and innovation within Apple. He encouraged cross-functional teams to work together on product development, and he personally reviewed and provided feedback on many of the company's products. He also encouraged open communication and debate within the company, which helped to generate new ideas and perspectives.

As with any major initiative, developing and executing a

successful strategy is not without its challenges. In fact, it is not uncommon to encounter unexpected obstacles or setbacks along the way. However, it is important to approach these challenges with a positive attitude and a willingness to learn and adapt.

Think about a challenge your organization has faced in relation to its strategy. Perhaps there was a major shift in the market that impacted your ability to achieve your goals, or maybe there was a misalignment between different departments or stakeholders that hindered progress. Whatever the challenge, take a moment to reflect on how you and your organization overcame it.

Consider the steps you took to address the challenge. Did you gather additional data or insights to better understand the problem? Did you bring in outside experts or consultants to provide a fresh perspective? Did you modify your strategy or adjust your goals to better align with the new reality?

It is also important to reflect on what you learned from the experience. Did the challenge reveal any weaknesses in your organization's processes or communication channels? Did it highlight the need for additional resources or skills? By taking a proactive approach to learning from challenges, you can identify areas for improvement and make adjustments to your strategy moving forward.

Remember, challenges are an inevitable part of any major initiative, but they can also be opportunities for growth and learning. By reflecting on past challenges and how you overcame them, you can develop the resilience and adaptability needed to successfully execute your organization's strategy in the future.

21

COMMON CHALLENGES

I n business, challenges are inevitable, and being able to anticipate and overcome them is crucial for success. Every business, regardless of its size, industry, or location, faces its unique set of challenges. However, some common challenges are ubiquitous across industries and affect all businesses, from startups to multinational corporations.

In the business context, the term "challenges" refers to any obstacles, difficulties, or problems that a company may face in achieving its objectives or goals. These challenges can come from both internal and external factors and can vary depending on the industry, company size, and other factors. Some common challenges that businesses may face include economic downturns, competition, changing market trends, regulatory issues, supply chain disruptions, technology disruptions, and talent management issues. Successfully navigating these challenges requires effective planning, communication, and execution strategies.

Kodak, a once-dominant player in the photographic film industry, faced a significant challenge executing its strategy when digital photography emerged. Despite being an early developer of digital cameras, Kodak's leadership was hesitant to embrace the new technology due to concerns about its potential impact on their lucrative film business. As a result, the company lost market share to competitors who quickly embraced the digital revolution. Kodak's failure to pivot their focus eventually led to their decline and bankruptcy in 2012. This serves as a prime example of the challenges companies face when adapting to technological disruption and shifting market trends (Anthony, 2016).

Common Challenges

Lack of Resources. Lack of resources typically refers to not having enough people, funding, equipment, or time to accomplish a task or pursue a strategy. It means that the resources required to achieve the goals of the business are not available, which can lead to difficulties and obstacles in executing a strategy. This can occur due to a variety of factors, such as poor financial planning, unexpected events, or changes in the market or industry. Without adequate resources, a company may struggle to achieve its objectives, compete effectively, or survive in the long term.

Resistance to Change. Resistance to change is a common human reaction to the introduction of a new idea, process, or technology that challenges established norms or ways of doing things. People are creatures of habit and tend to feel comfortable with familiar routines, so when faced with something new, they may feel uncertain, anxious, or even threatened. This can lead to resistance, which can take many forms, such as skepticism, negativity, reluctance, or even active opposition. Resistance to change can occur at any level of an organization, from entry-level employees to upper management, and can pose significant challenges to successfully implementing a new strategy or initiative. Understanding and managing resistance to change is a critical aspect of effective leadership and successful execution of strategy.

Lack of Alignment. Lack of alignment means that different parts of the organization are not working together towards the same goals or objectives. This can happen when there is a lack of communication or understanding about the organization's strategy, or when different parts of the organization have competing priorities or interests. When there is a lack of alignment, it can lead to confusion, inefficiency, and missed opportunities. For example, if the sales team is focused on generating revenue, while the product team is focused on creating new products, there may be tension and a lack of collaboration between the two teams. This can result in missed sales opportunities or products that do not meet the needs of customers. To overcome lack of alignment, it is important for organizations to have a clear and shared understanding of their strategy and objectives, and to create a culture of collaboration and communication across teams and departments.

Poor Communication. Poor communication refers to a situation where messages are not clearly and effectively transmitted between individuals or groups, resulting in misunderstandings, confusion, and potentially disastrous outcomes. In the context of executing a strategy, poor communication can occur at any level of an organization and hinder progress towards achieving strategic objectives. For example, leaders may fail to effectively communicate the importance of a particular initiative, leaving employees unsure of its significance or how to contribute to its success. Conversely, employees may have difficulty communicating challenges or concerns they encounter during execution, preventing leaders from making timely course corrections. In either case, poor communication can lead to delays, missed opportunities, and the failure to achieve strategic goals. To mitigate the risk of poor communication, it is important to establish clear lines of communication throughout an organization, provide training on effective communication strategies, and regularly solicit feedback to identify and address communication breakdowns.

Inadequate Measurement Tracking. Inadequate Measurement Tracking in the context of executing a strategy means not having an effective system to track and measure progress toward the goals of the strategy. This can happen when the metrics used to measure progress are not well-defined, not regularly monitored or reviewed, or not aligned with the goals of the strategy. When measurement tracking is inadequate, it can be difficult to determine whether progress is being made or if course corrections are needed. This can lead to a lack of accountability and alignment, as well as confusion and frustration among stakeholders. In order to avoid inadequate measurement tracking, it is important to establish clear and specific metrics, track progress regularly, and review results frequently to ensure that the strategy is on track.

Lack of Leadership and Commitment. Lack of leadership and commitment refers to a situation where the senior management of an organization fails to provide clear direction, support, and resources to ensure the successful execution of a strategy. In this scenario, executives may fail to fully communicate the importance of the strategy, may not provide the necessary resources, or may not model the desired behaviors.

Executing a strategy can be a challenging process for any business, and there are several common challenges that companies must navigate. These challenges can range from cultural resistance to change, lack of alignment among stakeholders, insufficient resources and expertise, and failure to adapt to changing market trends and technology. However, by recognizing these challenges and taking proactive steps to address them, companies can increase their chances of successfully executing their strategy and achieving their goals. This may include investing in employee training and development, establishing clear communication channels, prioritizing stakeholder engagement, and embracing a culture of innovation and continuous improvement. Ultimately, the key to overcoming common challenges in strategy execution is to remain agile, adaptable, and focused on the end goal, while also remaining responsive to the changing needs of the business and its stakeholders.

22

OVERCOMING CHALLENGES

I n the world of business, challenges are inevitable. From unexpected market shifts to internal organizational issues, companies must be prepared to overcome a variety of obstacles in order to succeed. Overcoming challenges is crucial for a company's long-term success, but it is not always an easy task. It requires careful planning, a willingness to adapt, and a strong sense of determination.

Businesses that ignore challenges can face negative consequences such as failure to achieve objectives, decreased productivity, financial losses, loss of reputation, reduced employee morale, and decreased stakeholder confidence. Ignoring challenges can lead to a lack of innovation and adaptability, which can make it difficult for the business to survive in a rapidly changing market. It is essential for businesses to proactively identify and address challenges in order to overcome them and remain competitive in their industry. By addressing challenges, businesses can learn from their mistakes, strengthen their processes and strategies, and ultimately improve their overall performance.

To effectively watch for challenges when executing a strategy, a leader should maintain open communication with their team and regularly assess the progress being made towards the goals of the strategy. This will help to identify any potential roadblocks or issues early on, which can then be addressed before they become bigger problems. It's also important for leaders to be proactive in addressing any challenges that do arise, and to work collaboratively with their team to find solutions. This might involve re-prioritizing tasks, reallocating resources, or adjusting timelines to better align with current circumstances.

In addition, a leader should regularly review the strategy and its execution with key stakeholders, such as employees, customers, and investors, to ensure that everyone is on the same page and aligned with the overall goals. This will help to identify any potential gaps or misalignments, and enable the leader to take corrective action as needed. Finally, leaders should maintain a growth mindset and be open to feedback and learning. By acknowledging and learning from past mistakes or challenges, they can develop new skills and strategies that will help to avoid similar issues in the future.

Domino's Pizza is a great example of a business that overcame a significant challenge and emerged even stronger. In the early 2010s, the company faced criticism from customers about the quality of its pizza, which threatened to damage its reputation and bottom line. However, rather than ignoring or denying the problem, Domino's embraced it as an opportunity to improve and innovate (Haden, 2021). Through a combination of marketing, operational changes, and customer engagement, the company was able to transform its negative perception into a positive one, resulting in increased sales and profits. This example highlights the importance of not only recognizing and addressing challenges but also approaching them with a proactive and solution-oriented mindset.

Starbucks' decline in the mid-2000s was a significant challenge for the company. The rapid expansion of stores led to a dilution of the brand and a decline in customer satisfaction. However, Starbucks' CEO Howard Schultz returned to the company in 2008 and implemented a series of changes to turn the business around. One of the first steps Schultz took was to close underperforming stores and reduce the number of new store openings, in order to refocus on the company's core products, such as coffee and espresso beverages.

Schultz also implemented a customer feedback program, which allowed the company to receive input from its customers and make changes based on their feedback. This feedback led to improvements in the quality of the coffee and the store atmosphere, which helped to improve customer satisfaction. Additionally, Schultz launched a comprehensive training program for employees, focusing on the company's core values and customer service. This helped to create a consistent experience for customers across all Starbucks locations, which further improved customer satisfaction.

Overall, Schultz's strategic changes helped to turn the tide for Starbucks. By focusing on the company's core products and improving customer service and satisfaction, Starbucks was able to overcome the challenge it faced and regain its position as a leading coffee retailer. Today, Starbucks continues to innovate and evolve, introducing new products and experiences to meet the changing needs and preferences of its customers.

- Acknowledge the challenge: The first step to overcoming any challenge is to acknowledge that it exists. This requires an honest assessment of the situation and the willingness to confront the problem head-on.
- Develop a plan: Once you have identified the challenge, it's important to develop a plan of action. This plan should include specific steps that can be

taken to address the challenge and a timeline for
implementation.

- Engage stakeholders: It's important to engage all
  relevant stakeholders in the process of overcoming a
  challenge. This includes employees, customers, and
  partners. It's important to listen to their feedback
  and involve them in the process of developing
  solutions.
- Stay focused on the long-term goal: It's important to
  stay focused on the long-term goal, even when
  facing challenges. This means not losing sight of the
  big picture and not getting sidetracked by short-
  term setbacks.
- Monitor progress: It's important to monitor progress
  and adjust the plan as needed. This requires
  ongoing evaluation and a willingness to make
  changes when necessary.
- Celebrate successes: Celebrating successes along the
  way can help to build momentum and keep
  everyone motivated. This can include recognizing
  individual achievements, team accomplishments,
  and overall progress towards the long-term goal.

Overcoming challenges when executing a strategy requires
a combination of planning, engagement, focus, flexibility, and
celebration. By following these tips, leaders can help their organizations stay on track and achieve their goals.

23

BEST PRACTICES FOR STRATEGY EXECUTION

Developing a winning strategy is only half the battle. The other half is executing it effectively. Strategy execution involves aligning resources, processes, and people to achieve strategic goals and objectives. Without effective execution, even the most brilliant strategy will fail to deliver the desired results.

Best practices refer to the most effective and efficient methods, processes, or techniques that have been proven to achieve a desired outcome. They are based on experience, research, and analysis and are widely accepted as the most effective way to perform a specific task or activity. Best practices provide a framework for decision-making and help organizations to standardize their processes and procedures.

In business, best practices can be used in a variety of areas, including strategy development, marketing, sales, customer service, operations, human resources, and more. They help organizations to achieve their goals by providing a blueprint for success, ensuring that all team members are working towards the same objectives, and avoiding common mistakes and pitfalls.

Examples of best practices in business may include implementing a customer relationship management (CRM) system to track customer interactions and improve customer service, regularly conducting performance evaluations and goal setting sessions to motivate employees and improve productivity, or using agile project management techniques to ensure projects are completed on time and within budget.

It's important to note that best practices are not set in stone and should be reviewed and adapted over time to ensure they remain relevant and effective. They should also be customized to meet the specific needs of an organization and the industry in which it operates.

Align Strategy and Operations

Aligning strategy and operations refers to the process of ensuring that the company's goals and objectives are reflected in its day-to-day activities and decision-making processes. This requires a clear understanding of the company's overall strategy, as well as an ability to translate that strategy into specific operational activities that will help achieve the desired outcomes.

Alignment can involve a range of activities, such as setting clear goals and performance metrics, ensuring that resources are allocated appropriately, developing processes and procedures that support the strategy, and creating a culture that encourages collaboration and innovation. By aligning strategy and operations, a company can ensure that everyone is working towards the same goals, which can increase efficiency, productivity, and overall performance. It can also help identify areas where there may be gaps or misalignments, allowing the company to make necessary adjustments to improve its execution of the strategy.

Establish Clear Goals and Objectives

Establishing clear goals and objectives means defining specific and measurable targets that an organization wants to achieve through the execution of its strategy. The goals and objectives should be aligned with the overall mission and vision of the organization, and they should be communicated clearly to all stakeholders, including employees, customers, and investors. Clear goals and objectives provide focus and direction, and they help to ensure that everyone is working toward the same objectives.

To establish clear goals and objectives, organizations should identify what they want to achieve, determine how they will measure progress, and set targets for performance. Goals and objectives should be specific, measurable, achievable, relevant, and time-bound (SMART), and they should be designed to support the overall strategy of the organization. The process of setting goals and objectives should involve input from all stakeholders, and it should be reviewed periodically to ensure that it remains relevant and aligned with the overall strategy of the organization.

Define Roles and Responsibilities

Defining roles and responsibilities is the process of clarifying the tasks, activities, and expectations for each individual or team involved in executing the strategy. This helps to ensure that everyone knows what they are responsible for, and that there is no confusion or duplication of effort. Defining roles and responsibilities also helps to establish accountability and promotes better collaboration between teams. It involves identifying key stakeholders, understanding their roles, and aligning their responsibilities to specific objectives. When roles and responsibilities are clearly defined, it is easier to track progress and identify areas that need improvement. This also helps to manage risks, identify dependencies, and avoid potential conflicts. Ultimately, it leads to greater efficiency, productivity, and the successful implementation of the strategy.

Communicate the Strategy

Communicating the strategy refers to the process of sharing the details of the strategy with the key stakeholders, including employees, investors, customers, suppliers, and other relevant parties. It involves providing a clear and concise explanation of the strategy's goals, objectives, and desired outcomes.

Communication of the strategy is essential for ensuring that all stakeholders are aware of what the company is trying to achieve, why it is important, and how it will be accomplished. Effective communication of the strategy helps to create alignment and buy-in from stakeholders, which is critical to the success of the execution of the strategy. It is also important to use various communication channels to reach different stakeholders, such as email, company newsletters, town hall meetings, video conferences, or social media platforms. The communication of the strategy should be ongoing and not limited to the initial launch of the strategy. It should be part of regular updates, progress reports, and discussions to ensure that everyone remains informed and engaged.

Establish a Process for Monitoring Progress

Establishing a process for monitoring progress is a critical step in executing a strategy. This involves developing a system to track and evaluate the performance of various initiatives and activities related to the strategy. The process should include identifying key performance indicators (KPIs) that are relevant to the strategy, establishing benchmarks and targets for those

KPIs, and determining how progress will be measured and reported.

The process should also include regular reviews and updates to the strategy as needed, based on the information collected through monitoring progress. This helps to ensure that the strategy remains relevant and effective, and that resources are being used efficiently.

Additionally, the process should involve communication and feedback loops to ensure that stakeholders are informed about progress, and to provide opportunities for input and course correction. This helps to build accountability and promote transparency, as well as to identify and address any challenges that arise during the execution of the strategy.

Foster a Culture of Accountability

Fostering a culture of accountability means creating an environment in which everyone is responsible for their actions, decisions, and outcomes. It means promoting a sense of ownership and pride in one's work and encouraging individuals to take initiative and be proactive. This involves defining clear expectations, providing feedback and recognition for good performance, and holding individuals and teams accountable for meeting their goals and objectives. It also involves establishing a process for reporting progress, identifying and addressing issues, and making necessary course corrections. A culture of accountability promotes transparency, trust, and a shared sense of purpose, and is essential for the successful execution of a strategy. When individuals and teams are held accountable for their actions, they are more likely to take ownership of the outcomes, take calculated risks, and find innovative solutions to challenges. This, in turn, helps to drive the organization's success and achieve its strategic objectives.

Continuously Review and Update the Strategy

Continuously reviewing and updating the strategy means that a company must regularly evaluate the effectiveness of its strategy execution and make adjustments as needed. The business environment is constantly changing, and a company's strategy must be adaptable to those changes to remain relevant and successful. Reviewing and updating the strategy involves monitoring progress against the established goals and objectives and assessing whether the current approach is delivering the desired outcomes. If progress is not being made, or if the business environment has changed significantly, the strategy may need to be revised or updated.

This process should involve input and feedback from various stakeholders, including employees, customers, and partners, to ensure that the strategy remains aligned with the company's mission and values. It also requires a willingness to learn from mistakes and make the necessary adjustments to improve performance. Regularly reviewing and updating the strategy is critical to ensure that the company remains agile and responsive to changing conditions, and to maintain a competitive advantage in the marketplace.

Executing a strategy successfully is crucial for the long-term success of any business. By following the best practices outlined above, businesses can increase their chances of successfully executing their strategies, and achieving their desired outcomes. It is important to remember that strategy execution is an ongoing process that requires constant monitoring and adjustments, and that setbacks and challenges may arise along the way. However, with a strong commitment to best practices and a willingness to adapt, businesses can overcome these challenges and achieve their strategic goals.

PART VII

SUSTAINING EXECUTION

If an organization is going to survive for over 100 years, it must have flexibility built into the strategy. 3M is a multinational conglomerate that I such a company. Founded in 1902, 3M started as a mining company before transitioning to manufacturing and diversifying into various other industries. One of the keys to 3M's longevity and success has been its ability to pivot and adapt to changing market conditions.

Embracing Innovation: 3M is known for its innovation and has a long history of developing new products and technologies. The company is committed to developing products that solve problems, improve lives, and make the world a better place. To achieve this goal, 3M encourages a culture of experimentation and risk-taking. The company provides its employees with the resources, support, and autonomy they need to explore new ideas and develop innovative solutions.

One example of 3M's innovative culture is the invention of waterproof sandpaper. In the early 1920s, sandpaper was made from paper and glue, and it would break down quickly when exposed to water. This was a significant problem for the auto industry, as workers needed sandpaper that could withstand water to sand down the metal parts of cars. To solve this problem, 3M developed a waterproof sandpaper that was made from silicon carbide grit and waterproof adhesive. The new product was a game-changer for the auto industry, as it allowed workers to sand down metal parts even when they were wet.

This innovative culture has led to numerous breakthroughs over the years. 3M has developed products such as Post-it Notes, Scotch tape, reflective sheeting, and abrasives, among others. These products have not only solved problems but have also created new markets and industries. For example, Post-it Notes were originally developed as a solution for keeping bookmarks in place, but they have since become a ubiquitous office supply that is used around the world.

Innovation is deeply ingrained in 3M's culture, and the company continues to invest heavily in research and development to develop new products and technologies. Through its commitment to innovation and experimentation, 3M has been able to pivot and adapt to changing market conditions and maintain its position as a leader in numerous industries.

Diversifying its Product Portfolio: 3M is a highly diversified company with a broad product portfolio that spans multiple industries. The company operates in areas such as healthcare, transportation, consumer goods, and electronics. This diversification has been a key factor in the company's success and longevity, allowing 3M to weather economic downturns and adapt to changing consumer trends.

By operating in multiple industries, 3M is not overly dependent on any one market or customer. This diversification helps the company mitigate risks and reduces its exposure to fluctuations in any one industry. For example, during economic downturns, demand for some of 3M's products in one industry may decrease, but the company's presence in other industries can help offset these losses.

Moreover, 3M's diversified product portfolio enables the company to stay ahead of changing consumer trends. By having a wide range of products, 3M can respond quickly to changes in consumer preferences and needs. The company can also cross-sell products and leverage its diverse capabilities to create new products and services that cater to emerging market needs.

For example, 3M's healthcare division offers a broad range of products such as medical tapes, dressings, and wound care products. Meanwhile, the transportation division produces automotive products such as adhesives and tapes for automotive assembly, graphic films for vehicle wraps and signage, and automotive coatings. By operating in multiple industries, 3M has been able to develop a deep understanding of different markets and customers, enabling it to innovate and stay ahead of the curve.

In summary, 3M's diversified product portfolio has been a key factor in the company's success. By operating in multiple industries, 3M has been able to weather economic downturns and adapt to changing consumer trends. This diversification has also enabled the company to cross-sell products and leverage its capabilities to create new products and services that cater to emerging market needs.

Focusing on Sustainability: In recent years, 3M has recognized the importance of sustainability and environmental responsibility and has made a concerted effort to integrate these principles into its business operations. The company has set ambitious goals to reduce its environmental footprint and has made significant progress in areas such as energy efficiency, waste reduction, and sustainable sourcing.

One of 3M's key sustainability goals is to reduce its greenhouse gas emissions by 50% by 2030. To achieve this goal, the company has implemented a number of initiatives, such as improving energy efficiency in its manufacturing facilities, increasing the use of renewable energy sources, and investing in new technologies to reduce emissions.

Additionally, 3M has committed to reducing waste by implementing sustainable manufacturing practices and investing in recycling and waste reduction programs. The company has also set targets for reducing water usage and has implemented measures to ensure that it sources materials and products from sustainable and responsible suppliers.

In addition to these internal efforts, 3M has also introduced a range of environmentally sustainable products. For example, the company has developed a line of Post-it Notes made from recycled paper and adhesives that are derived from plant-based materials. 3M has also introduced a range of environmentally friendly packaging solutions that are designed to reduce waste and minimize environmental impact.

3M's sustainability efforts have not only helped the company reduce its environmental footprint but have also improved its reputation and appeal to consumers who are increasingly concerned about sustainability and ethical business practices. By prioritizing sustainability, 3M has demonstrated its commitment to creating a more sustainable future and has positioned itself as a leader in responsible business practices.

Investing in Research and Development: 3M is known for its strong emphasis on research and development (R&D), which has been a key factor in the company's success. 3M invests heavily in R&D, with a significant portion of its budget allocated towards developing new products and technologies.

The company has a robust R&D division, which is responsible for identifying new market opportunities, conducting research on emerging technologies, and developing innovative products that meet customer needs. 3M's R&D division is spread across multiple locations globally and employs thousands of researchers and scientists who work on various projects.

Over the years, 3M's investment in R&D has paid off in the form of numerous breakthroughs and innovations. Some of the most notable products developed by the company include the first waterproof sandpaper, Scotch tape, and Post-it notes, which have become household names around the world.

3M's R&D efforts have also resulted in significant advancements in areas such as adhesives, coatings, and optical films, which have helped the company expand its product portfolio and enter new markets.

By investing heavily in R&D, 3M has been able to maintain a competitive edge in an ever-changing business landscape. The company's focus on innovation has helped it stay ahead of the curve, adapt to changing market trends, and develop new products that meet evolving customer needs.

Prioritizing Customer Needs: 3M places a strong emphasis on understanding its customers' needs, which has been a key factor in the company's success. The company recognizes that to develop products and solutions that meet customer needs, it is essential to have a deep understanding of the challenges and pain points that customers face.

To gain this understanding, 3M conducts extensive research to identify customer pain points and gather feedback on its products and services. This research is conducted through various channels, including customer surveys, focus groups, and direct interaction with customers.

Based on the insights gathered through customer research, 3M develops new products and solutions that address specific customer needs. The company's product development process is iterative, with multiple rounds of prototyping and testing to ensure that the final product meets customer requirements.

In addition to developing new products, 3M also places a strong emphasis on improving its existing products to better meet customer needs. The company regularly solicits customer feedback on its products and uses this feedback to identify areas for improvement.

For example, when developing a new line of Post-it Notes, 3M conducted extensive research to understand how customers use the product and what features were most important to them. The company used this information to develop a new line of Post-it Notes with improved adhesive and increased durability, which better met the needs of its customers.

By placing a strong emphasis on understanding its customers' needs, 3M has been able to develop products and solutions that are highly valued by its customers. This has helped the company maintain a loyal customer base and position itself as a leader in innovation and customer-centricity.

~

Using the Four Levers of Control framework, developed by Robert Simons, we can evaluate how companies such as 3M employed a flexible approach to pivot and adapt to changing circumstances over the years. The framework provides a holistic approach to management, allowing organizations such as 3M to establish control mechanisms that can be flexibly adjusted based on changing circumstances.

For example, as 3M has pivoted over the years to expand into new markets and focus on sustainability. The belief systems lever has helped the company establish a culture of innovation and risk-taking, while the boundary systems lever has helped ensure that employees operate within ethical and legal boundaries.

Meanwhile, the diagnostic control systems lever has allowed 3M to monitor and measure its performance in areas such as R&D and sustainability, while the interactive control systems lever has facilitated communication and collaboration among employees across the organization.

By viewing the success through the lens of the Four Levers of Control framework, we see how 3M has been able to pivot and adapt to changing circumstances, while also maintaining the discipline and structure necessary to execute its strategy effectively. The framework shows us that flexibility is necessary for organizations that need to pivot and evolve over the years while also ensuring that its employees remain aligned with the company's values, mission, and vision.

Flexibility is an important component of any successful strategy, as it allows organizations to adapt to changing circumstances and weather disruptions. Take a moment to reflect on your organization's strategy and consider whether you perceive it as flexible.

Ask yourself the following questions:

If a disruption were to occur, do you believe your organization's strategy would be able to weather the storm? For example, if there was a sudden shift in the market or a major supplier went out of business, would your strategy be resilient enough to survive?

Do you believe your organization's strategy is nimble enough to pivot if necessary? Can your organization respond quickly to new opportunities or challenges, and make changes to the strategy as needed?

If you answered "no" to either of these questions, it may be time to consider making adjustments to your organization's strategy to increase its flexibility. This could involve developing contingency plans for potential disruptions, or creating processes to regularly review and adjust the strategy as new information becomes available.

However, if you answered "yes" to both questions, congratulations! Your organization's strategy may already be well-positioned to weather disruptions and adapt to changing circumstances. It is important to continue to monitor and assess the strategy's flexibility over time to ensure it remains effective in the face of new challenges.

Remember, flexibility is key to long-term success, and being able to pivot and adapt to changing circumstances can help your organization stay ahead of the curve and maintain a competitive advantage.

24

EMBEDDING THE CULTURE INTO THE ORGANIZATION'S DNA

Culture is a crucial aspect of any organization, shaping the behavior, values, and attitudes of its employees. A positive and effective culture can drive performance, innovation, and collaboration, while a negative culture can hinder progress and lead to dissatisfaction among employees. Therefore, it is essential for organizations to embed the right culture into their DNA to achieve success in the long run.

One of the main challenges that businesses face when balancing long-term goals with short-term gains is the temptation to prioritize short-term gains at the expense of long-term success. This can happen because short-term results are often more tangible and immediately rewarding, while the benefits of investing in longer-term goals may take years to materialize. However, if a business is overly focused on short-term gains, it may sacrifice its long-term growth and competitiveness.

Another challenge is the need to balance competing priorities. For example, a business may need to invest in research and development to remain competitive in the long term, but it also needs to allocate resources to meet immediate customer demands and maintain profitability. Finding the right balance between these competing priorities requires careful planning, prioritization, and communication.

Additionally, businesses may face external pressure from stakeholders, such as investors, who may prioritize short-term gains over long-term growth. This can make it difficult for a business to balance short-term and long-term goals, particularly if it is under pressure to deliver immediate returns.

In order to effectively balance short-term gains with long-term goals, businesses need to develop a clear strategy that outlines both short-term and long-term objectives. They also need to establish clear metrics for tracking progress towards both sets of goals and ensure that they are communicating progress to stakeholders on a regular basis. Finally, they need to cultivate a culture that prioritizes long-term thinking and encourages employees to embrace the company's long-term vision.

Amazon is a company that is renowned for its innovative and customer-centric approach to business. However, this approach has not always been easy, as Amazon has had to make difficult decisions that sacrificed short-term gains for long-term goals. One such decision was made in the early days of the company when Amazon invested heavily in growth and expansion, resulting in significant losses in the short term. This move was not popular with investors, as the company's stock price plummeted. However, Amazon's founder and CEO, Jeff Bezos, believed that investing in the company's long-term growth and customer experience was the key to success (Chaffey, 2022).

By focusing on long-term goals, Amazon was able to build a loyal customer base and expand into new markets and business areas, such as cloud computing and artificial intelligence. This approach has paid off handsomely, as Amazon is now one of the world's most valuable companies, with a market capitalization of over $1 trillion. This example serves as a testament to the power of a long-term focus on strategy and execution, even if it requires sacrificing short-term gains.

Tesla's commitment to long-term goals and willingness to prioritize them over short-term profits has been a driving force behind the company's success (Lobo, 2020). While other car companies were hesitant to invest in electric cars due to the high cost and limited demand, Tesla took a bold approach, believing that electric cars could become mainstream with the right technology and infrastructure. By sticking to this vision, Tesla not only disrupted the traditional car industry but also paved the way for a more sustainable future.

In addition to its innovative products, Tesla's success can also be attributed to its strategic investments in other areas such as battery technology and renewable energy. By expanding beyond the electric car market, Tesla has positioned itself as a leader in the transition to sustainable energy, which is becoming increasingly important in today's world.

Embedding a culture of strategy execution into a company's DNA requires a long-term vision and ongoing effort from leadership and management.

- Lead by example: Company leaders should model the behavior they expect from others. They need to consistently prioritize the company's strategy and hold themselves accountable for executing it.
- Communicate the strategy clearly and consistently: Ensure that every employee understands the company's strategy, goals, and objectives. Communicate the strategy regularly through various channels such as meetings, emails, and newsletters.
- Align goals and objectives: Align individual goals and objectives with the company's strategy. Make sure that each employee knows how their work contributes to the overall success of the company.

- Foster collaboration: Encourage collaboration between departments and teams. Foster an environment where people are comfortable working across teams and are empowered to make decisions.
- Celebrate successes: Celebrate the successes along the way, no matter how small. Recognize and reward employees who are making an effort to execute the strategy.
- Continuously review and update the strategy: Regularly review the company's strategy and update it as necessary. Solicit feedback from employees and stakeholders to ensure that the strategy is relevant and effective.

Embedding the culture into an organization's DNA is crucial for long-term success. It is not only about defining values and behaviors but also about consistently reinforcing them through actions, communications, and incentives. Companies that prioritize culture have a better chance of attracting and retaining top talent, improving performance, fostering innovation, and building a strong brand reputation. To embed the culture effectively, organizations must involve all stakeholders, from senior leaders to front-line employees, and continuously monitor and adjust their approach to align with changing business needs and external trends. By making culture a priority and ensuring that it is deeply ingrained in every aspect of the organization, companies can create a sustainable competitive advantage and achieve their strategic objectives.

25

CONTINUOUS IMPROVEMENT

Continuous improvement is a critical aspect of any successful organization. It refers to the ongoing effort to improve processes, products, and services in response to changing customer needs, market trends, and internal inefficiencies. By continuously refining their operations, organizations can increase efficiency, reduce costs, and enhance their competitive advantage.

The goal of continuous improvement is to make incremental, sustainable improvements that add value and enhance quality. This involves identifying opportunities for improvement, analyzing processes to determine root causes of problems, and implementing changes to address those root causes. Continuous improvement can involve a variety of methodologies, such as Lean, Six Sigma, Kaizen, and Total Quality Management, among others.

Continuous improvement originated in the manufacturing industry in Japan, specifically with the Toyota Motor Company. In the 1950s, Toyota developed the Toyota Production System, which emphasized continuous improvement as a key component. The system was designed to increase efficiency and eliminate waste in manufacturing processes. Over time, continuous improvement has been adopted in various industries and has become a widely used business practice. Continuous improvement is a process that involves constantly reviewing and refining your business practices to achieve better results.

- Set clear goals: Define your business objectives and the metrics you will use to measure success.
- Analyze your current processes: Identify areas where you can make improvements to streamline operations, increase efficiency, and reduce waste.
- Identify opportunities for improvement: Look for ways to optimize your processes, such as by introducing new technology or eliminating unnecessary steps.
- Implement changes: Introduce changes to your business processes that will improve your operations and help you achieve your goals.
- Measure results: Track your progress against your goals and analyze the impact of your changes. Use data to identify areas for further improvement.
- Continuously improve: Make continuous improvement a part of your business culture by encouraging feedback and empowering your employees to suggest changes.

Continuous improvement is an ongoing process that requires dedication and commitment, but the rewards can be significant in terms of improved efficiency, increased productivity, and better customer satisfaction.

Postmortems

Postmortems, also known as retrospective analysis, have been used in businesses for many years. Postmortems refer to the analysis of a project, process, or event after it has been completed to identify what went well, what didn't, and how the organization can improve in the future.

The use of postmortems in the business world became more widespread in the 1990s, particularly in the tech industry. This was due in part to the rise of agile methodologies, which emphasize continuous improvement and feedback. Postmortems were seen as a valuable tool for identifying areas of improvement and promoting a culture of learning and growth within organizations.

Since then, postmortems have become a popular practice in many industries, from software development to finance to healthcare. They are now considered an essential part of many organizations' continuous improvement processes, helping teams to learn from their mistakes and make better decisions in the future.

Postmortems can be a valuable tool in developing your business strategy by helping you identify areas for improvement and opportunities for growth.

- Identify the event or project to review: Choose a significant event or project that has recently taken place in your business, such as a product launch, marketing campaign, or major change in operations.
- Gather data: Collect data and feedback from individuals involved in the event or project, including timelines, communications, actions taken, and outcomes.
- Analyze the data: Use the data collected to identify the root causes of any issues or challenges that

occurred during the event or project. This will help you understand what worked well and what needs to be improved.

- Identify opportunities for improvement: Based on your analysis, identify specific areas for improvement in your business strategy, such as changes to processes, procedures, or systems.
- Develop an action plan: Develop an action plan for implementing the changes identified in the postmortem. Assign responsibility for each action item and set a timeline for completion.
- Follow-up: Monitor progress on the action plan and adjust your strategy as needed based on feedback and results.

By using postmortems in your business strategy development, you can learn from past events and projects, identify areas for improvement, and develop a more effective strategy for your business. This can help you to reduce the risk of future failures and increase your chances of success.

26

CELEBRATING SUCCESS AND LEARNING FROM FAILURE

C elebrating success and learning from failure are two essential aspects of business that can make or break an organization's success. While success is often celebrated, failures are often viewed as setbacks and something to be avoided at all costs. However, it's important to recognize that failures can also provide valuable lessons and insights that can help organizations improve and succeed in the long run. Celebrating success and learning from failure are two sides of the same coin, and organizations that can strike a balance between the two are often the most successful.

Celebrating success in business means acknowledging and recognizing achievements and milestones that are significant to the business. It involves taking the time to acknowledge the hard work and efforts of the individuals and teams involved in achieving success, and creating a positive and rewarding culture within the organization.

Celebrating success can have several benefits, such as boosting morale and motivation, reinforcing values and goals, encouraging continued success, attracting and retaining talent, and fostering collaboration and teamwork. By recognizing the

hard work and achievements of individuals and teams, celebrating success can help to create a positive and supportive
work culture where employees feel valued and appreciated. It
can also help to create a shared sense of purpose and direction
within the organization by highlighting examples of success
that align with the values and goals of the organization. Additionally, celebrating success can help to encourage individuals
and teams to continue striving for success, creating a culture of
continuous improvement and growth. This can help to differentiate the organization from competitors, increase employee
loyalty and engagement, and foster collaboration and teamwork by recognizing the contributions of individuals and
teams. Overall, celebrating success is an important tool in
building a successful business.

- Recognizing individual and team achievements:
  This can be done through formal recognition
  programs, such as employee of the month awards or
  bonuses, or through informal recognition, such as a
  simple thank-you or a shout-out during a team
  meeting.
- Holding team celebrations: This can involve team
  outings, dinners, or other activities that allow team
  members to socialize and bond outside of work.
- Sharing success stories: This can involve sharing
  stories of success with the wider organization, such
  as through company newsletters, social media, or
  presentations.
- Giving back to the community: Celebrating success
  can also involve giving back to the community, such
  as through charitable donations or volunteer work.

Google has a program called "gThanks" that allows
employees to send a message of thanks and recognition to their

colleagues for their contributions. Google also has a "Peer Bonus" program where employees can nominate each other for a monetary bonus for outstanding work. In addition, the company celebrates major milestones such as product launches and anniversaries with parties and special events. Google's approach to celebrating success has helped to create a positive and rewarding work culture, where employees feel valued and appreciated, and motivated to continue striving for success.

Learning from Failure

Failure is an inevitable part of any business journey, and the way organizations approach and learn from failure can make a significant impact on their future success. While success stories often grab headlines, learning from failure is equally important for achieving sustainable growth and staying ahead of the competition. In fact, some of the world's most successful companies, such as Amazon, Apple, and Google, have experienced failures along the way and have used them as opportunities to learn, innovate, and improve.

Learning from failures is a critical component of organizational growth. It involves taking a constructive and analytical approach to understanding and analyzing the reasons behind unsuccessful outcomes or mistakes. Rather than simply dismissing a failure, organizations can use it as a valuable learning opportunity to identify what went wrong, why it happened, and what can be done to prevent similar failures in the future. The process of learning from failures involves several key steps, including acknowledging and analyzing the failure, identifying areas for improvement, developing a plan for improvement, implementing the plan, and monitoring progress. By adopting a growth mindset and using failures as opportunities for learning and growth, organizations can develop resilience, build confidence, and create a culture of continuous improvement and learning. Overall, learning from failures is essential for organizational development, and can lead to increased adaptability and innovation in the face of challenges.

SpaceX has had several high-profile failures in its efforts to develop reusable rockets and send payloads into space. For example, in 2015, a Falcon 9 rocket carrying supplies to the International Space Station exploded shortly after liftoff. In 2016, another Falcon 9 rocket exploded during a test on the launch pad.

However, rather than being discouraged by these failures, SpaceX has used them as learning opportunities to improve its processes and technology. After each failure, SpaceX has conducted extensive investigations to understand the root causes of the problem and implement corrective actions. For example, after the 2015 explosion, SpaceX identified a design flaw in one of the rocket's fuel tanks and made changes to prevent the problem from happening again.

SpaceX's willingness to learn from its failures has enabled it to make significant progress in the field of space exploration. In 2017, the company successfully launched and landed a used Falcon 9 rocket, marking a major breakthrough in the development of reusable rockets. In 2020, SpaceX also successfully launched astronauts into space for the first time, making history as the first private company to do so.

Celebrating success and learning from failure are both important to a business strategy because they help to create a culture of continuous improvement and learning, which can drive innovation, growth, and long-term success. Celebrating success can help to boost morale, build confidence, and create a sense of shared purpose and achievement among employees. It can also reinforce positive behaviors and outcomes, and help to align individual and team goals with the broader goals of the organization.

Learning from failure is equally important because it provides valuable insights into what works and what doesn't, and can help to identify areas for improvement and growth. By analyzing the reasons behind failures, individuals and organizations can develop a deeper understanding of their strengths and weaknesses, and identify opportunities to optimize their processes and strategies. This can lead to increased efficiency, productivity, and innovation, and can also help to mitigate risks and prevent future failures.

Incorporating both celebrating success and learning from failure into a business strategy can create a culture of continuous improvement and learning, where success and failure are seen as opportunities for growth and development. This can help organizations to adapt quickly to changing market conditions, stay ahead of the competition, and achieve long-term success.

PART VIII

USING THE FRAMEWORK

The four levers of control framework can be a useful tool when developing a strategy for your organization. Here are some ways you can use the framework:

Belief Systems: Start by defining your company's values, mission, and vision. These should be the foundation for your strategy and should guide the behavior and decision-making of your employees. Make sure your belief systems are clear, concise, and communicated effectively throughout your organization.

- What are the core values and mission of our organization?
- How do these values and mission align with the goals and objectives of our strategy?
- How can we effectively communicate these beliefs to our employees?

Boundary Systems: Establish rules and procedures that set the limits of acceptable behavior for your employees. This includes ethical and legal boundaries, as well as guidelines for how work is done within the organization. Make sure these boundaries are well-defined and communicated effectively to all employees.

- What are the ethical and legal boundaries we need to establish to guide employee behavior?
- What guidelines should we have in place to ensure consistent work practices and quality standards?
- How can we ensure that these boundaries are clearly communicated to all employees?

Diagnostic Control Systems: Develop measures and metrics that allow you to monitor and control performance. This includes financial metrics, as well as non-financial metrics related to customer satisfaction, employee engagement, and other key performance indicators. Use these metrics to track progress toward your strategic goals and make adjustments as necessary.

- What are the key performance indicators (KPIs) we need to monitor to ensure that we are meeting our strategic goals?
- How can we effectively track and measure progress toward these KPIs?
- How can we use this data to identify opportunities for improvement and make necessary adjustments to our strategy?

Interactive Control Systems: Establish communication channels that facilitate dialogue and feedback among employees. This includes regular team meetings, feedback sessions, and other opportunities for employees to share ideas and provide input. Make sure these channels are open and accessible to all employees, regardless of their position within the organization.

- How can we foster open communication and collaboration among employees?
- What feedback mechanisms should we have in place to ensure that employees feel heard and valued?
- How can we use this feedback to improve our strategy and operations?

Overall, the four levers of control framework can help you establish a strategy that is well-aligned with your company's values, mission, and vision, while also providing a structure for monitoring and adjusting performance over time. By leveraging this framework, you can develop a strategy that is flexible, adaptive, and effective in achieving your long-term goals.

As you reflect on your own organization's strategy, you may be wondering if implementing the four levers of control would be beneficial. Here are some questions to consider:

First, do you have a clear understanding of your organization's belief systems? Are these beliefs aligned with your organization's strategy, and are they communicated effectively throughout the organization?

Second, do you have effective boundary systems in place to guide decision-making and ensure that your organization stays on track? Do you have clear policies and procedures in place to prevent deviations from the strategy?

Third, do you have effective diagnostic control systems to monitor and evaluate performance? Are you collecting the right data to track progress towards your goals, and are you using this information to make informed decisions?

Finally, do you have effective interactive control systems in place to foster communication and collaboration across the organization? Are you engaging stakeholders at all levels to ensure that everyone is aligned around the strategy and working together to achieve the organization's goals?

If you answered "no" to any of these questions, it may be worth considering implementing the four levers of control to help improve your organization's strategic management. By incorporating these levers, you can create a more structured approach to strategy implementation, which can increase the likelihood of success and help your organization achieve its goals.

However, it's important to note that every organization is different, and what works for one may not work for another. Before implementing any new strategy or management model, it's important to carefully consider the unique needs and characteristics of your organization, and to seek input from all stakeholders to ensure buy-in and support.

27

MANAGING TENSION

The successful execution of a business strategy is crucial for any organization's growth and sustainability. However, executing a strategy is not without its challenges, particularly when it comes to balancing short-term goals with long-term objectives. The tension of strategy execution refers to the balancing act that companies must navigate to ensure they are achieving immediate results while also investing in future growth and innovation. While short-term gains can be tempting, a focus on immediate results can lead to the neglect of long-term goals and hinder a company's ability to adapt to changing market conditions. Managing this tension effectively requires a strategic approach that prioritizes both short-term performance and long-term vision.

Managing the tension of strategy execution also involves balancing the interests and needs of different stakeholders, such as shareholders, employees, customers, and the community. For example, meeting short-term financial targets may please shareholders, but it could lead to cost-cutting measures that harm employee morale or compromise the quality of products or services. Conversely, investing in long-term growth and innovation may benefit employees and customers in the long run, but it may require sacrificing short-term profits or taking on more risk.

Additionally, managing the tension of strategy execution requires adaptability and flexibility, as organizations must be able to adjust their plans and tactics in response to changing circumstances or unexpected challenges. For example, a sudden economic downturn or a disruptive new competitor could require a shift in priorities or a new approach to strategy execution.

Managing the tension of strategy execution is a complex and ongoing challenge for organizations, and it requires a strategic mindset, effective communication, and a willingness to learn from both successes and failures. By navigating this tension effectively, organizations can achieve their goals while also building a strong foundation for future success.

Utilizing the Four Levers of Control framework can help leaders balance the need for long-term strategy and short-term gains by providing a structured approach to managing the organization's resources. By defining the organization's belief system, establishing boundary systems, implementing diagnostic control systems, and creating interactive control systems, leaders can ensure that the organization remains focused on its long-term goals while also making progress towards short-term objectives.

As discussed in Chapter 5, Strategy Execution involves striking a delicate balance between different aspects of an organization's systems. On one hand, the Belief Systems and Interactive Control Systems provide a wide range of opportunities for growth and innovation. On the other hand, the Boundary Systems and Diagnostic Controls offer a necessary level of focus and discipline to ensure that the organization stays on track towards its goals. Achieving this balance is essential for successful Strategy Execution, as it requires leveraging both the creative potential and the disciplined approach within the organization. It is the Yin and Yang of Strategy Execution.

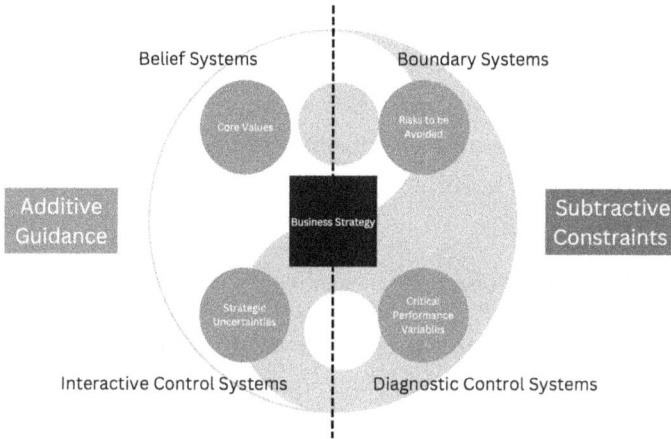

The Balance Within the Four Levers of Control

Define your Belief System

As discussed earlier, effective strategy execution requires a balance between belief systems and interactive control systems on the left and boundary systems and diagnostic controls on the right. Your organization's belief system is composed of its values, culture, and mission, which should guide your strategic decisions and actions. To align your strategy with your organization's core principles, values, and purpose, you need to first clarify your belief system. This involves identifying your organization's values, cultural norms, and mission. By doing so, you can make better strategic decisions that reflect your organization's identity and mission.

For instance, a company that prioritizes short-term profits over long-term sustainability and social responsibility may face negative consequences, such as reputational damage, customer backlash, and legal issues. To improve their belief systems, the company can ask questions to identify areas of improvement, such as understanding their impact on the environment and society, shifting their focus towards a more balanced approach, engaging with stakeholders, and ensuring that their beliefs and values are reflected throughout the company. By reflecting on their belief systems, the company can take action to align their actions and decisions with their values and goals, leading to a more sustainable and responsible approach that can benefit the company in the long run.

Establish your Boundary Systems

Boundary systems are an essential part of strategy execution, as they define the acceptable behavior and actions within an organization. To establish effective boundary systems, it is necessary to consider the organization's values, culture, and mission. This ensures that policies and procedures align with the belief system and help achieve strategic objectives. For instance, a company that values honesty and transparency may implement policies requiring open communication and internal audits.

In practice, companies often face challenges with communication breakdowns, inconsistent processes, and collaboration issues, especially when they expand operations to multiple locations. Such challenges can be addressed by improving boundary systems. To do so, companies may ask questions such as: What are the current communication channels, and are they effective for all teams and locations? Are there any areas of overlap or duplication of efforts that can be streamlined? What processes can be implemented to ensure consistency in quality of work across all locations? By addressing such questions, companies can establish better boundary systems, ensuring consistency in processes and collaboration across all locations.

Implement Diagnostic Control Systems

Diagnostic control systems are a set of measures that help you monitor and evaluate your organizational performance in alignment with your strategic objectives. To establish effective diagnostic control systems, you should first define your strategic goals and objectives. Then, you need to identify the key performance indicators (KPIs) that are relevant to your objectives. For instance, if your objective is to boost revenue, your KPIs may include sales growth, customer acquisition rate, and customer retention rate.

After identifying the KPIs, you need to establish a monitoring and tracking system, which may include regular reporting, data analysis, and performance reviews. By using diagnostic control systems, you can track your performance, identify areas of strength and weakness, and make informed decisions.

For example, let's consider ABC Corporation, a manufacturing company that has been experiencing delays in their delivery schedule and quality control issues resulting in high defective products. After reviewing their diagnostic control systems, ABC Corporation realized the need for improvement in this area.

To improve their diagnostic control systems, ABC Corporation may ask questions such as:

- How can we better analyze and track our production data to identify inefficiencies and areas for improvement?
- Are we using the right metrics to measure quality and efficiency in our production process?
- How can we empower our employees to identify and solve production issues?

- Are we leveraging the right tools and technology to support our production process?
- How can we better align our production goals with our overall business strategy?

By addressing these questions and enhancing their diagnostic control systems, ABC Corporation can improve their production process, minimize inefficiencies and errors, and ultimately provide better outcomes for their customers.

Create Interactive Control Systems

Interactive control systems refer to communication and feedback processes that aid in learning and adapting while implementing a strategy. These systems should foster open and honest communication, encourage collaboration, and enable the identification of improvement opportunities.

To establish interactive control systems, start by creating regular channels of communication between stakeholders and team members, such as meetings, progress reports, and feedback sessions. Build a culture of transparency and respect to promote open and honest communication. Use feedback to identify areas where the strategy needs improvement and make adjustments accordingly.

Consider the example of a software company that is facing a decline in customer satisfaction and sales. Upon investigating, they discover that their customer service representatives are failing to provide effective solutions to customer complaints. To enhance their interactive control systems, the company may ask the following questions:

- How can we improve the training and development of our customer service representatives to handle customer complaints better?

- Are we regularly collecting and analyzing customer feedback? If not, how can we establish a system to do so?
- How can we incentivize our customer service representatives to provide better solutions for customer complaints?
- Do our current customer service policies and procedures require revision or are they effective?

By addressing these questions and implementing changes, the company can strengthen their interactive control systems and boost customer satisfaction and sales. They can ensure that their customer service representatives are equipped to handle complaints effectively, gather and analyze feedback, incentivize employees to provide better solutions, and regularly review and update their policies and procedures.

28

FLEXIBILITY & BALANCE

The framework of Four Levers of Control emphasizes the significance of balancing control and flexibility in an organization's strategy implementation. According to this model, organizations can attain balance by employing four different types of control: belief systems, boundary systems, diagnostic control systems, and interactive control systems.

Flexibility is a critical element in an organization's ability to respond to market changes and leverage emerging opportunities. Belief systems and interactive control systems act as the foundation for flexibility by empowering employees to make decisions and fostering innovation. On the other hand, boundary systems and diagnostic control systems provide the necessary structure and discipline to ensure that the organization remains focused on achieving its goals and objectives.

The importance of balance between these four levers of control can be illustrated through the example of Apple. Apple has a strong belief system, including a mission to provide innovative and easy-to-use products. This belief system has been consistent throughout the company's history, and has allowed

Apple to develop products that are highly differentiated from its competitors. Apple's interactive control system, which fosters creativity and collaboration among its employees, has been critical in enabling the company to continuously innovate and create new products.

At the same time, Apple's boundary and diagnostic control systems have provided the necessary structure and discipline to ensure that the company remains focused on its goals. For example, Apple's strict quality control processes have helped the company maintain a high level of customer satisfaction and loyalty. Apple's success can be attributed to its ability to balance flexibility and control through effective use of the four levers of control.

~

COLECO, short for Connecticut Leather Company, was founded in 1932 and originally produced leather products such as wallets and belts. In the 1950s, the company shifted its focus to plastic and metal products, including toys and novelties.

Coleco's biggest success came in the 1980s with the release of its Cabbage Patch Kids dolls. The dolls quickly became a cultural phenomenon, and Coleco struggled to keep up with the high demand. However, in the mid-1980s, the popularity of the dolls waned, and Coleco was left with excess inventory and declining sales.

To pivot and try to recapture its success, Coleco shifted its focus to electronic gaming. In 1982, it released the highly successful tabletop arcade game, Donkey Kong, which was licensed from Nintendo. Coleco followed up with other successful gaming products such as the ColecoVision console and the handheld electronic game line called "Head to Head."

Unfortunately, Coleco's success in the gaming market was short-lived. The video game market crashed in 1983, and Coleco's sales dropped significantly. The company attempted to diversify again by entering the computer market with the Adam computer, but it was plagued with technical issues and production delays, ultimately resulting in its failure.

Overall, Coleco's ability to pivot from leather products to toys and eventually to electronic gaming demonstrates the importance of adapting to changing markets and consumer demands in order to remain competitive. However, it also highlights the risks involved in pivoting too quickly or without proper planning, as evidenced by the failure of the Adam computer.

～

IBM (INTERNATIONAL BUSINESS MACHINES) was originally founded in 1911 as the Computing-Tabulating-Recording Company (CTR) and primarily manufactured punched card machines used for data processing. Over the years, IBM evolved into a leading provider of mainframe computers and software, with a focus on serving large enterprises.

In the 1980s, IBM faced a significant challenge as the personal computer market emerged, threatening its core mainframe business. Rather than resisting the trend towards personal computing, IBM decided to pivot its strategy and focus on developing and selling personal computers. This led to the creation of the IBM PC, which became a major success and helped IBM to remain a major player in the technology industry.

However, in the early 1990s, IBM faced another challenge as the personal computer market became increasingly commoditized and competitive. To address this challenge, IBM pivoted once again and shifted its focus towards providing technology services and consulting, which had higher margins and were less subject to commoditization. This shift in strategy proved successful, and today IBM is a leading provider of enterprise technology services and consulting.

Through these pivots, IBM remained true to its core strategy of providing technology solutions to large enterprises, but adapted to changing market conditions and customer needs. By doing so, IBM was able to stay ahead of the curve and remain a major player in the technology industry for over a century.

29

EXAMPLES OF FAILED STRATEGY
EXECUTION

S tudying the failures of organizations in strategy
execution is crucial for various reasons. Firstly, examining the errors of such organizations enables us to
learn from their mistakes and avoid repeating them, enhancing
the effectiveness of our strategies and increasing the likelihood
of success. Secondly, exploring the failures of these organizations helps us identify the challenges they faced when implementing strategies, enabling us to develop more practical plans
that account for potential obstacles. Thirdly, studying multiple
failures allows us to recognize common pitfalls and challenges
that often arise in executing strategies, helping us to proactively
address these issues and avoid making the same errors. Finally,
analyzing the failures of organizations helps us identify areas
where our own organization may be falling short, allowing us
to develop strategies to address these issues and enhance our
performance. While a variety of reasons can lead to organizational failure, such as weak leadership, poor financial management, or lack of customer focus, each company's path to
success or failure is unique and may depend on a range of

196   JAMES G. SMITH

factors. Therefore, it is essential to dig deeper to uncover the underlying issues that led to these strategic misses.

Kodak

Kodak was a leading company in the film-based photography industry for most of the 20th century. However, as digital photography emerged in the 1990s, Kodak faced a significant challenge to its core business. In 1975, Kodak engineer Steve Sasson invented the world's first digital camera, but Kodak's leadership failed to see the potential of this technology and instead continued to focus on its traditional film-based business.

By the time Kodak realized the significance of digital photography and attempted to shift its focus to this technology, it was already too late. Kodak's rivals had already established a significant presence in the digital photography market, and Kodak was unable to keep up. The company declared bankruptcy in 2012.

One of the key reasons for Kodak's failure was a lack of strategic focus and a failure to execute a successful strategy. Despite being the inventor of digital photography, Kodak was unable to capitalize on this technology due to its lack of strategic vision and an unwillingness to cannibalize its core business. The company's leadership was slow to adapt to the changing market and failed to invest in new technologies that could have helped Kodak maintain its competitive advantage.

In contrast, Kodak's competitors, such as Canon and Sony, were able to execute successful strategies by quickly adopting digital photography and investing heavily in research and development to improve their products. By doing so, they were able to gain a significant competitive advantage over Kodak and ultimately drive it out of business.

The failure of Kodak can be analyzed through the Four

Levers of Control framework. Kodak's business model was built around the traditional photographic film, which was the mainstay of its business for many decades. However, the advent of digital photography disrupted Kodak's business model, and the company was unable to adapt to this change.

Belief Systems. Kodak's belief systems were centered around the belief that the photographic film would remain the dominant form of photography. The company had invested heavily in research and development to improve the quality of photographic film. However, the belief system failed to recognize the shift towards digital photography and the importance of investing in digital technology.

Boundary Systems. Kodak's boundary systems failed to identify the threats posed by digital photography, and the company did not take any measures to address these threats. Kodak failed to recognize the emergence of new competitors and was not able to respond to the changing market conditions.

Diagnostic Control Systems. Kodak's diagnostic control systems failed to monitor the changing market trends and to identify the risks posed by digital photography. The company was not able to react quickly to changes in the market and was slow to invest in digital technology.

Interactive Control Systems. Kodak's interactive control systems failed to encourage communication and collaboration between different departments. The company was not able to bring together its research and development and marketing departments to create new digital products.

Kodak's failure was due to a lack of flexibility and balance in its strategy. The company was too focused on its traditional business model and failed to recognize the importance of digital technology. Kodak's strategy failed to adapt to the changing market conditions and the company was unable to pivot its business model to digital photography.

Blockbuster

Blockbuster was a major player in the video rental industry in the late 1990s and early 2000s, with thousands of stores across the United States and other countries. However, the company failed to adapt to the rise of online streaming and home delivery services such as Netflix and Redbox.

Blockbuster initially attempted to compete by launching its own online rental service, but it was not successful due to high costs and technical issues. The company also failed to recognize the shift in consumer preferences from physical media to digital media, and did not invest in developing its own streaming service or partnerships with existing streaming providers.

Blockbuster Video's strategy was mainly focused on diagnostic control systems and boundary control systems. Their emphasis was on controlling their operations and reducing costs by using metrics like revenue, inventory turnover, and store-level profitability. They were also primarily focused on maintaining their existing business model of renting physical DVDs and had a limited belief in the potential of online streaming. This narrow focus on short-term financial performance at the expense of innovation and long-term sustainability ultimately led to their downfall.

The Four Levers of Control framework highlights the importance of balancing all four control systems, including interactive control systems and belief systems. Interactive control systems allow for collaboration and learning, whereas belief systems focus on fostering a shared vision and values that guide decision-making.

In the case of Blockbuster, their lack of interactive control systems led to a lack of collaboration and learning. They did not invest enough in digital technology and were slow to adapt to the changing market. Additionally, their belief system did not support innovation and adaptation to new trends, as they were too focused on their existing business model.

As a result, when streaming services like Netflix emerged, Blockbuster was unable to compete and ultimately filed for bankruptcy in 2010. This highlights the importance of a balanced approach to the Four Levers of Control framework, as relying too heavily on diagnostic and boundary control systems can lead to a lack of adaptability and ultimately harm a company's long-term prospects.

Sears

Sears, founded in 1892, was a retail powerhouse that dominated the American retail landscape for much of the 20th century. At its peak in the 1970s, Sears was the largest retailer in the world and a symbol of American consumerism. However, the company struggled to adapt to the changing retail landscape in the 21st century.

Sears faced intense competition from other retailers, such as Walmart and Target, which offered lower prices and a wider selection of products. In addition, the rise of e-commerce giants like Amazon made it more difficult for Sears to compete. The company struggled to keep up with these changes and was slow to invest in e-commerce and other new technologies.

Sears, once the largest retailer in the United States, is an example of a company that failed to balance the Four Levers of Control framework effectively.

Belief Systems. Sears had a long-standing reputation as a trustworthy and reliable brand, which was reinforced through its extensive catalogue sales and robust customer service. However, as the retail landscape changed, the company failed to adapt its beliefs to new consumer preferences, which included a shift towards online shopping and an increased focus on experiences rather than products.

Interactive Control Systems. Sears had a weak interactive control system, which refers to the company's ability to respond to changing market conditions in real-time. The company was slow to adopt e-commerce and digital marketing strategies, which limited its ability to compete with online retailers like Amazon. Additionally, the company's management was notorious for being siloed, which prevented effective communication and collaboration between different departments.

Boundary Systems. In terms of boundary systems, Sears struggled to maintain its competitive advantage as the retail landscape became increasingly crowded and competitive. The company failed to identify and respond to the threat posed by online retailers like Amazon, and as a result, lost market share to more innovative and agile competitors.

Diagnostic Control Systems. Sears had weak diagnostic control systems, which refers to the company's ability to measure and monitor its performance against its strategic goals. The company failed to leverage data and analytics effectively, which limited its ability to make informed decisions and improve its operations. Additionally, the company's financial performance suffered due to years of mismanagement and underinvestment.

The company was slow to adapt to changing consumer preferences and market conditions, which limited its ability to remain competitive and relevant. Additionally, the company's management was resistant to change and failed to leverage data and analytics effectively, which prevented the company from making informed decisions and improving its operations.

Nokia

Nokia is a notable example of a company that failed to execute a successful strategy in response to a rapidly changing market. At the beginning of the 21st century, Nokia was the world's largest vendor of mobile phones, with a market share of over 40%. The company had a strong presence in both developed and emerging markets and was widely respected for its technology and innovation.

Nokia is a classic example of a company that failed to adapt to changing market conditions and ultimately lost its dominance in the mobile phone industry. Using the Four Levers of Control framework, we can examine how Nokia's failure can be explained by its inability to maintain a balance across all four levers.

Belief Systems. Nokia's dominant belief system was that it was the world's leading mobile phone manufacturer, and that its superior technology and design would keep it ahead of competitors. However, this belief was not grounded in the reality of shifting consumer preferences and the emergence of new smartphone competitors like Apple and Samsung.

Boundary Systems. Nokia's boundary systems were rigid and bureaucratic, which made it difficult for the company to respond quickly to changes in the market. The company had a large, centralized decision-making structure that made it slow to adapt to emerging trends.

Diagnostic Control Systems. Nokia relied heavily on financial metrics to measure success, such as revenue and profit margins. This focus on short-term financial performance may have led Nokia to overlook longer-term trends and invest too little in research and development to keep pace with competitors.

Interactive Control Systems. Nokia did not effectively engage with external stakeholders, such as consumers and developers, to understand their needs and preferences. This lack of interaction made it difficult for Nokia to stay ahead of emerging trends and respond to changing market conditions.

Taken together, Nokia's failure can be seen as a result of an imbalance across all four levers of control. The company's rigid belief system and boundary systems made it difficult to adapt to new trends, while its focus on short-term financial metrics and lack of interaction with stakeholders made it difficult to stay ahead of emerging competitors. Ultimately, Nokia's inability to maintain a balance across all four levers of control led to its decline and eventual sale of its mobile phone business.

30

EXAMPLES OF SUCCESSFUL STRATEGY EXECUTION

S tudying organizations that succeed at strategy execution is also important for several reasons. By examining the strategies and practices of successful organizations, we can learn from their best practices and adopt them in our own organizations. This can help us improve our chances of success and achieve better results. Also, studying successful organizations can help us benchmark our own organizational performance against industry leaders. By identifying areas where we need to improve, we can set targets for improvement and work towards achieving them.

Amazon

Amazon's strategy can be summarized as customer-centric, innovation-driven, and diversified.

Customer-centric: Amazon's focus is on the customer, and it aims to provide the best possible customer experience. This includes offering a wide range of products, fast and reliable delivery, competitive prices, and excellent customer service.

Innovation-driven: Amazon has a strong focus on innovation, and it continually strives to develop new and improved products and services. This includes investing heavily in research and development, experimenting with new technologies such as AI and machine learning, and expanding into new markets and industries.

Diversified: Amazon has diversified its business portfolio to include a wide range of products and services, from e-commerce and cloud computing to streaming services and advertising. This diversification allows Amazon to leverage its strengths across different industries and create new revenue streams.

Overall, Amazon's strategy revolves around providing the best possible customer experience, continually innovating and expanding into new markets, and diversifying its business portfolio to create new revenue streams.

Diagnostic Control Systems. Amazon has established various metrics and key performance indicators (KPIs) to measure its performance and guide decision-making. For instance, Amazon tracks customer satisfaction, inventory turnover, and delivery times to ensure that it meets its customers' expectations.

Boundary Control Systems. Amazon has a strong focus on its customer-centric culture and has set strict policies and standards for its suppliers and partners to maintain that focus. This has enabled Amazon to build trust with its customers, which has translated into loyal customer base.

Belief Systems. Amazon's core values of customer obsession, ownership, and long-term thinking drive its decision-making processes. For example, its customer obsession value ensures that the company always prioritizes the customer experience above all else.

Interactive Control Systems. Amazon promotes open communication and collaboration among its employees through various channels such as meetings, forums, and social media platforms. This encourages employees to share ideas and feedback, which helps the company to continuously improve and innovate.

By effectively utilizing all four levers of control, Amazon has been able to maintain its focus on delivering exceptional customer experiences, while also achieving long-term growth and profitability.

Toyota

Toyota's strategy is focused on continuous improvement, innovation, and quality. The company aims to provide high-quality vehicles at affordable prices while maintaining its position as a global leader in the automotive industry. Toyota's strategy is based on the Toyota Production System, which emphasizes the elimination of waste, the promotion of lean manufacturing, and the use of continuous improvement processes.

The company's core values, including respect for people, teamwork, and customer focus, are also fundamental to its strategy. Toyota has a strong commitment to sustainability and has set ambitious goals to reduce its carbon footprint and promote environmental responsibility. The company is also focused on developing innovative new technologies, such as electric and hybrid vehicles, to meet the changing demands of the automotive market.

Overall, Toyota's strategy is centered on a strong focus on quality, efficiency, innovation, and sustainability, while maintaining a customer-centric approach. This approach has enabled the company to maintain a competitive edge in the global automotive industry and build a strong brand reputation for quality and reliability.

Belief Systems. Toyota's belief system is centered around the concept of "Kaizen," which translates to continuous improvement. The company places a strong emphasis on teamwork, employee empowerment, and customer focus. Toyota encourages its employees to constantly seek out opportunities to improve processes and eliminate waste, leading to a culture of continuous improvement.

Boundary Systems. Toyota maintains strong relationships with its suppliers and dealers, working closely with them to ensure that quality standards are met and that the supply chain operates efficiently. Toyota also sets high standards for safety and environmental responsibility, using its boundary systems to enforce these standards throughout its operations.

Diagnostic Control Systems. Toyota uses a range of diagnostic control systems to monitor and improve its production processes. For example, the company uses a system called "Andon" to identify production issues in real-time and address them immediately. This system allows for quick identification of problems and prevents defects from being passed down the production line.

Interactive Control Systems. Toyota places a strong emphasis on training and development, providing employees with the skills and knowledge needed to effectively carry out their roles. The company also uses interactive control systems to encourage collaboration and communication among employees. For example, the "Obeya" system is used to facilitate cross-functional communication and decision-making, allowing for faster and more effective problem-solving.

Overall, Toyota's success can be attributed to its focus on continuous improvement, strong relationships with suppliers and dealers, effective diagnostic control systems, and emphasis on employee training and collaboration. By leveraging all four levers of control, Toyota has been able to build a highly efficient and innovative organization that consistently delivers high-quality products to its customers.

Starbucks

Starbucks' strategy is focused on providing a premium coffee experience to its customers, while also offering a welcoming and comfortable environment in its coffee shops. The company's core values include a commitment to quality, social responsibility, and innovation.

One key aspect of Starbucks' strategy is its focus on creating a unique and consistent customer experience across all of its locations. This includes the use of high-quality ingredients, well-trained baristas, and a comfortable and inviting atmosphere in its coffee shops.

Another aspect of Starbucks' strategy is its focus on sustainability and social responsibility. The company has implemented a number of initiatives to reduce its environmental impact, such as using renewable energy, reducing waste, and sourcing sustainable coffee beans. Starbucks also supports local communities through various social programs, such as the Starbucks Foundation, which funds education, community service, and disaster relief projects.

In terms of growth, Starbucks has pursued a strategy of expansion through opening new stores in both domestic and international markets. The company has also diversified its product offerings to include food, tea, and other beverages, as well as merchandise such as mugs and tumblers.

Overall, Starbucks' strategy is centered on providing a premium coffee experience, while also prioritizing social responsibility and sustainability, and pursuing growth through expansion and diversification of its product offerings.

Interactive Control Systems. Starbucks uses interactive controls to ensure that its employees provide excellent customer service. The company invests heavily in employee training to ensure that every customer interaction is a positive experience. The interactive controls used by Starbucks also ensure that customers receive their orders promptly and accurately. The company has developed a mobile app that allows customers to place orders in advance, and pick them up without having to wait in long lines.

Belief Systems. Starbucks has a strong belief system that emphasizes the importance of ethical sourcing and sustainability. The company sources its coffee beans directly from farmers and pays them a fair price. Starbucks also implements sustainable practices, such as using recyclable materials in its stores and minimizing waste. This belief system has helped the company build a strong brand image and attract customers who value ethical and sustainable practices.

Boundary Systems. Starbucks uses boundary systems to ensure consistency across its stores. The company has strict standards for store design, menu offerings, and customer service. This ensures that customers have a consistent experience at any Starbucks location they visit. The company also uses boundary systems to protect its brand by enforcing strict rules on the use of its logo and trademarks.

Diagnostic Control Systems. Starbucks uses diagnostic controls to monitor and improve its performance. The company tracks key metrics, such as customer satisfaction, store sales, and employee turnover, to identify areas for improvement. Starbucks also uses technology, such as point-of-sale systems and customer data analytics, to track customer preferences and behavior.

Starbucks' success can be attributed to its ability to balance the Four Levers of Control. The company uses interactive controls to ensure excellent customer service, belief systems to promote ethical and sustainable practices, boundary systems to maintain consistency, and diagnostic controls to monitor and improve performance. By executing its strategy well, Starbucks has built a strong brand image and a loyal customer base, which has enabled it to remain a leader in the coffee industry.

AFTERWORD

After reading this book on strategy execution, you now understand that a solid strategy is just the beginning. The real challenge lies in executing that strategy and turning it into tangible results. You've learned that successful execution requires a combination of effective leadership, clear communication, alignment of resources, and continuous monitoring and adaptation.

The stories and case studies in this book have demonstrated the importance of being agile and flexible in executing strategies. They have shown that even the best strategies can fail without proper execution. However, they have also shown that with the right approach, even struggling organizations can turn things around and achieve great success.

Remember that strategy execution is a continuous process. It's not a one-time event but rather an ongoing effort that requires constant attention and adaptation. Don't be afraid to course-correct and make adjustments as needed. Embrace the challenges and obstacles that come your way as opportunities to learn and improve.

As you move forward with executing your organization's

strategy, keep in mind the key lessons from this book. Focus on building a strong foundation of leadership and communication, aligning resources and capabilities, monitoring progress and adapting as needed. By doing so, you'll be well on your way to turning your strategy into reality and achieving the results you desire. Good luck!

BIBLIOGRAPHY

Anthony, S. D. (2016, Jul 15). *Kodak's Downfall Wasn't About Technology.* Retrieved from Harvard Business Review: https://hbr.org/2016/07/kodaks-downfall-wasnt-about-technology

Beheshti, N. (2018, Oct 5). *Remembering Steve Jobs: A Visionary Leader Who Changed The World.* Retrieved from Forbes: https://www.forbes.com/sites/nazbeheshti/2018/10/05/remembering-steve-jobs-a-visionary-leader-who-changed-the-world/?sh=6b6600e4ced7

Butler, J. (2022, Aug 24). *90 Percent of Organizations Fail to Execute Their Strategies Successfully: A White Paper to Help You Avoid Being a Statistic.* Retrieved from IntelliBridge: https://www.intellibridge.us/90-percent-of-organizations-fail-to-execute-their-strategies-successfully/

Chaffey, D. (2022, May 25). *Amazon.com marketing strategy 2022: E-commerce retail giant business case study.* Retrieved from Smart Insights: https://www.smartinsights.com/digital-marketing-strategy/online-business-revenue-models/amazon-case-study/

Cote, C. (2020, Nov 17). *5 Keys to Successful Strategy Execution.* Retrieved from Harvard Business School Online: https://online.hbs.edu/blog/post/strategy-execution

Disney. (n.d.). *About.* Retrieved from The Walt Disney Company: https://thewaltdisneycompany.com/about/

Freeland, G. (2020, Feb 24). *Indra Nooyi's Passions: People, Performance & Purpose At PepsiCo And Beyond.* Retrieved from Forbes: https://www.forbes.com/sites/grantfreeland/2020/02/24/indra-nooyis-passions-people-performance--purpose-at-pepsico-and-beyond/?sh=5077d926457c

Freiberg, K., & Freiberg, J. (2019, Jan 4). *20 Reasons Why Herb Kelleher Was One Of The Most Beloved Leaders Of Our Time.* Retrieved from Forbes: https://www.forbes.com/sites/kevinandjackiefreiberg/2019/01/04/20-reasons-why-herb-kelleher-was-one-of-the-most-beloved-leaders-of-our-time/?sh=19c32c0ab311

Haden, J. (2021, Jan 14). *10 Years Ago, 'Cardboard' Pizza Almost Killed Domino's. Then, Domino's Did Something Brilliant.* Retrieved from Inc.: https://www.inc.com/jeff-haden/10-years-ago-cardboard-pizza-almost-killed-dominos-then-dominos-did-something-brilliant.html

Heathfield, S. M. (2021, Feb 17). *Find Out How Zappos Reinforces Its Company*

Culture. Retrieved from liveabout: https://www.liveabout.com/zappos-company-culture-1918813

Husain, S., Khan, F., & Mirza, W. (2014, Sep 28). *How Starbucks pulled itself out of the 2008 financial meltdown*. Retrieved from Business Today: https://www.businesstoday.in/magazine/lbs-case-study/story/how-starbucks-survived-the-financial-meltdown-of-2008-136126-2014-09-22

Kaplan, R. S., & Norton, D. (2005, Oct). *The Officer of Strategy Management*. Retrieved from Harvard Business Review: https://hbr.org/2005/10/the-office-of-strategy-management

Neilson, G. L., Karla, L. M., & Elizabeth, P. (2008, Jun). *The Secrets to Successful Strategy Execution*. Retrieved from Harvard Business Review: https://hbr.org/2008/06/the-secrets-to-successful-strategy-execution

Lobo, A. (2020, Mar 24). *A case study on Tesla, Inc : The world's most exciting Automobile company*. Retrieved from Medium: https://medium.com/@ashleylobo98/a-case-study-on-tesla-the-worlds-most-exciting-automobile-company-535fe9dafd30

PMI. (2013). *Why Good Strategies Fail: Lessons for the C-suite*. Retrieved from IntelliBridge: https://www.intellibridge.us/90-percent-of-organizations-fail-to-execute-their-strategies-successfully/

Richwine, L., & Adegoke, Y. (2011, Sep 19). *Netflix splits DVD and streaming services*. Retrieved from Reuters: https://www.reuters.com/article/us-netflix/netflix-splits-dvd-and-streaming-services-idUSTRE78I23B20110919

Sellers, P. (2015, Nov 10). *How Coke Is Kicking Pepsi's Can (Fortune, 1996)*. Retrieved from Fortune: https://fortune.com/2015/11/10/coca-cola-pepsi-fortune-1996/

Simons, Robert. (Revised May 2018.) "Strategy Execution Module 15: Using the Levers of Control to Implement Strategy." Harvard Business School Module Note 117-115, December 2016.

Simons, Robert. (1995) 'Control in the Age of Empowerment', Harvard Business Review, 73, 2, pp.80-88

Wiles, J. (2021, Apr 26). *The 5 Pillars of Strategy Execution*. Retrieved from Gartner: https://www.gartner.com/smarterwithgartner/the-five-pillars-of-strategy-execution

ABOUT THE AUTHOR

James G. Smith is an accomplished business leader and coach with over 20 years of experience. He holds a Master of Business Administration, a Bachelor of Business Management, and a certification of Strategy Execution from Harvard Business School.

When James is not working, he enjoys exploring the Rocky Mountains, which he calls home. He is an avid hiker and enjoys spending time in nature with his family.

www.ingramcontent.com/pod-product-compliance
Lightning Source LLC
Chambersburg PA
CBHW071557210326
41597CB00019B/3286